WHO ARE WE?

MIPELA EM HUSAT?

EXPLORING TRADITIONAL KNOWLEDGE, SKILLS AND RESOURCES IN PAPUA NEW GUINEA

Stephen Ranck

OXFORD

OXFORD
UNIVERSITY PRESS

Oxford University Press is a department of the University of Oxford. It furthers the University's objective of excellence in research, scholarship, and education by publishing worldwide. Oxford is a registered trademark of Oxford University Press in the UK and in certain other countries.

Published in Australia by
Oxford University Press
253 Normanby Road, South Melbourne, Victoria 3205, Australia

First published 2014

ISBN 978 0 19 552237 2

Edited by Owen Salter
Illustrated by Birdwing PNG
Typeset by Kerry Cooke, eggplant communications
Printed in China by Golden Cup Printing Co. Ltd

With grateful acknowledgment of contributions from Jennifer Litau, Ila Geno, Radi Riri Warakai and Anthony Lilou

CONTENTS

CHAPTER 5

TRADITIONAL APPROACHES TO RESOURCES

CHAPTER 6

TRADITIONAL CONSERVATION

CHAPTER 7

TRADITIONAL SOLUTIONS FOR CONFLICT

CHAPTER 8

USING TRADITIONAL KNOWLEDGE TO HELP A COMMUNITY PROJECT

WHO ARE WE? MIPELA EM HUSAT?

As a society and as individuals, Papua New Guineans ask, 'Who are we?' or 'Who am I?' How much of us comes from traditional or community knowledge? This textbook helps you find answers to these questions.

This book is about exploring traditional and community knowledge concerning who we are. It shows you how you can link this to your school studies. It is an exciting area to explore. And like everything in Papua New Guinea, it is an area that is changing.

There is knowledge all around you. It does not matter if you are urban or rural. Anywhere in Papua New Guinea you will be able to investigate knowledge held by the community. You will be able to look deeper into who you are.

THE CHANGES AROUND YOU

Papua New Guinea is changing. The change is rapid. New people are coming into the country. New roads are being built for resources. Aeroplanes are full of business travellers. Billions of kina are being invested in oil and gas resources. Money for mining and other businesses is also coming into the country. The impact is felt all over the nation.

Papua New Guinea is open to globalisation. Students must study hard to find a place in the global economy. New skills and knowledge are needed. There are opportunities and there are many problems.

You can explore where traditional knowledge and values can help people with changes. You can also explore where such knowledge and values do not help.

Does the city represent a different Papua New Guinea, full of imported goods and ideas? Or can you find traditional knowledge, ideas and values at work here?

Is the village the seat of unchanged tradition? Or is it impacted by new ideas, goods and services? What does the village future hold for these two Sepik children?

THE IMPACT OF CHANGE ON PEOPLE

Sometimes it seems like there are two or more Papua New Guineas. One has offices, mines, pipelines, trips to very big stores, big business and big money. The other has little money, gardens, *tok ples*, sing sings, and trips to the forest or *big bus* to collect clan resources.

In one Papua New Guinea people speak English, learn to read and write in school, and study things like economics, mathematics and sciences. In the other Papua New Guinea people speak *tok ples* or Tok Pisin, learn from elders and parents, and study by doing things.

Some people feel like they have started to cross a bridge between the two Papua New Guineas. Now they are stuck in the middle. They cannot go back. They have trouble going forward. They begin to ask who they are.

The purpose of this textbook is to look at these questions. Who are we? What is our future? What is our past?

ABOUT THIS BOOK

The focus of this textbook is on traditional knowledge and how it links to your school studies. This is a supplementary text to help students and teachers explore knowledge in their communities.

Each community and each person will be different. The textbook will give you examples and show you how to explore ideas. You will find your own answers. You will find places where there are links between what you learn at school and what people learn in communities. You may also find places where there are no links.

You will be able to explore ways to make links stronger or weaker.

The examples in this text are intended to supplement other parts of the curriculum. You do not have to follow every section. You can flip through the text to find areas of interest applied to parts of the curriculum where you have extra time. You may use examples and techniques from this book for your studies in other fields such as science, English and maths.

THE CURRICULUM AND THIS TEXT

By law, teachers and schools must follow the National Education Department's curriculum. This supplementary text follows the social science curriculum for Grades 9 and 10. There are links to many other subjects.

Any teacher or student who wants to explore traditional knowledge in other parts of the curriculum can use this text as a model. It shows how to approach the different subjects. Many of the examples in the text could be transferred to other supplemental studies.

NAMES FOR KNOWLEDGE AND SKILLS

What do we call knowledge held by the community? The peoples of Papua New Guinea have been building knowledge for thousands of years. There are different names for this. It can be called:

- traditional knowledge
- folk knowledge
- indigenous knowledge
- local knowledge
- community knowledge.

This is the knowledge, ideas and skills that communities use in everyday life. You may also explore some knowledge or skills that are rarely used today but that form part of the history of how things were once done. That fits into the history part of the social science curriculum.

The name is not so important. You can decide what you want to call it. The knowledge has grown and changed over time. Knowledge in Papua New Guinea continues to change. You can become a knowledge explorer.

TRICKY WORDS

There is some bias in English in the words used about traditional knowledge. The word 'traditional' may imply something old or less useful. It is often compared with the word 'modern', which implies something new and better.

But everything traditional was modern once. New traditions are created all the time.

So we must think carefully about the words we use. We must look for bias. You will explore different terms. You will decide what helps people and what hurts people. You can explore what traditions to keep and what new traditions need to be created.

LOOK AHEAD

Traditions change. Cultures change. Communities change. And so does their knowledge. These are all things you can explore. You can discover:

- What types of knowledge exist in a community?
- Who keeps the knowledge?
- What is the knowledge about?
- How does it relate to your life?
- How does it relate to your school studies?

Community knowledge may explain activities differently from your school studies. You will want to look at the different explanations. Different knowledge systems may give different reasons why something happens or works.

Understanding differences can help you understand communities. Often people in communities will have knowledge of their environment that has not been recorded. You may help preserve knowledge by recording community knowledge that is now disappearing. There is a small section at the back of this textbook to show you how you can help preserve community knowledge for the future (see pages 113–15.).

You will be able to compare community knowledge to the knowledge you are learning at school. The next eight chapters follow the social science curriculum for Grades 9 and 10. Grades 9 and 10 each have four units of study. Each unit is a chapter in this book. Each chapter in this text gives examples of traditional knowledge linked to the study units. Here is an outline of the approach.

Teachers, you will see that some of this material could be used in earlier units in Grades 6, 7 or 8 if you modify it to learning levels at those grades.

CORRELATION CHART: INDIGENOUS KNOWLEDGE AND THE SOCIAL SCIENCE GRADE 9 AND 10 SYLLABUS

Chapter	Indigenous knowledge topic	Correlation to Social Science Grade 9 and 10 syllabus	Things you might explore
1	Traditional knowledge of the land around us	Grade 9 Social Science Unit 1: Places in the Pacific region	• Local ideas and stories about landforms • Dealing with natural hazards • Connections between the land, vegetation and climate • How human beings use the land
2	Tradition and people on the move	Grade 9 Social Science Unit 2: Population change, resources and migration	• The interaction between land and people • Traditional approaches to growing populations and their impacts on the land • Traditional practices taken into urban environments • Traditional links between rural and urban environments
3	Traditional knowledge of the past	Grade 9 Social Science Unit 3: Investigating Papua New Guinea history	• The history of your local area
4	Traditional leadership and civics	Grade 9 Social Science Unit 4: Civics and citizenship	• How did traditional leadership work in the past? And how does this influence the present? • What were traditional ethics or values for leaders and followers? What use have these now? Do they help or stop PNG being a strong nation?
5	Traditional approaches to resources	Grade 10 Social Science Unit 1: Resource development and management	Traditional and community knowledge about: • renewable and non-renewable resources • changes to resources and resource use
6	Traditional conservation	Grade 10 Social Science Unit 2: Environmental change, pollution and solutions	Traditional and community knowledge about: • the local environment and ways to use it • protecting the environment • conservation and preservation of the environment

(continues)

Chapter	Indigenous knowledge topic	Correlation to Social Science Grade 9 and 10 syllabus	Things you might explore
7	Traditional solutions for conflict	Grade 10 Social Science Unit 3: Papua New Guinea and the global community	• Traditional knowledge about conflict and fighting • Traditional solutions for conflict inside a family: how to settle differences in families, especially traditional solutions for domestic violence • Traditional solutions for conflict inside a community: how to settle differences between clans or families • Traditional solutions for conflict between communities: how to settle differences between traditional enemies
8	Using traditional knowledge to help a community project	Grade 10 Social Science Unit 4: Think globally, act locally	• This is your choice. See examples at the end of the book.

LINKING TRADITIONAL KNOWLEDGE TO OTHER PARTS OF THE CURRICULUM

You may wish to explore traditional knowledge in other areas of the curriculum. You can look for science, social science and maths knowledge any time you go into a community. All major community activities will have some maths, social science and science to them.

SCIENCE

Knowledge in science comes from observation and experimentation. This is called *empirical knowledge*. Science builds and tests theories using empirical knowledge. Obviously Papua New Guinea people have been observing and experimenting for thousands of years. This is the basis for local science.

You can find examples of local science all around you. One example is mumu stones (below).

MUMU STONES

Mumu stones are piled in a circle for heating. The circle is made like a cone. The imaginary point of the cone would be deep in the ground. A fire is built inside the stone circle. The stones are sloped slightly outward. After an hour or two the stone circle collapses. The mumu maker knows the stones are now hot enough to cook food.

Science explains the stones falling down by expansion from heat. When the stones have enough stored heat from the fire, they expand. This causes them to collapse.

MATHEMATICS

Knowledge in mathematics comes from reasoning and experiments. All traditional PNG societies had number systems. They also had different ways to measure and estimate. You may wish to explore these ideas along with the maths you are studying in Grades 9 and 10.

ENGLISH: COMPARATIVE STUDY

Language is covered in this book in Chapter 2 on migration. Comparing English with other languages used in Papua New Guinea may help you better understand English and the different parts of grammar that make up languages. Traditional stories, myths and legends can all be compared with any literature taught.

HERE IS A PUZZLE

Traditional knowledge is based on oral communication and teaching by doing. As soon as you start to study it from school, you are mixing imported knowledge with traditional knowledge. Photographs, radio broadcasts, videos, books, other written material and school reports all come from imported knowledge. They are all non-traditional. How do the two fit together? Do they influence each other? Are they creating a new Papua New Guinea tradition?

TRADITIONAL KNOWLEDGE OF THE LAND AROUND US

Unit 1 Grade 9 compares your local geography with the geography of other places in the Pacific Region.

For the traditional community, the land includes everything above it, below it and in it. The land is at the heart of much traditional knowledge. This includes the coastal sea. In this chapter, you start to explore people's knowledge of their land and how to thrive on it.

There are a number of places in the unit where you might explore traditional or community knowledge and ideas about the land. These include:

- how land is shaped
- dealing with natural hazards
- connections between the land, vegetation and climate
- land use.

HOW LAND IS SHAPED

This section is about landforms. Mountains, islands, lagoons, rivers and plains are all examples of landforms. There are traditional ideas and stories about how some of these formed. You could collect ideas about how they were created by giant creatures or people in the past. This could also link to Chapter 3 on local history.

Some ideas about landforms may involve ways to protect people. There are dangers associated with some landforms. Traditionally, people had knowledge about dealing with natural hazards.

For example, a Sepik woman who lived near a deep stream might warn children about this place. She might tell them about a gigantic snake that lived in the stream. The idea was that it swallowed people whole. Just telling children, 'Be careful, the stream is deep and you could drown', was not as strong a warning. The more frightening idea of a giant, human-swallowing snake might make a child take more care about this hazard.

Other stories about dangerous landforms are similar. Swamps are an example. There are traditional stories about spirits in underwater canoes that can grab people at night in the swamps.

LANDFORMS AND DEFENCE

Traditional warfare often had people considering defence. Settlements might use landforms for defence. For example, a ridge settlement or a hilltop settlement is easier to defend than an open beach. Can you find any other traditional use of landforms for defence in times of war?

CREATION TALES ABOUT LANDFORMS

There are many stories that explain how a landform came to be. Here is one example involving some special islands. They are officially known as the Davapia Rocks, but locally they are called the Beehives (below).

THE BEEHIVES

The Beehives are unusual islands in Simpson Harbour, Rabaul. Science explains them as part of a large volcano. Local stories explain them as marking the place of a fight.

Science explains that the harbour is part of a large volcano that was created by two major eruptions. These happened 3100 and 1400 years ago. There have been many smaller eruptions since. The Beehives are from one of the smaller eruptions. They are what is left of a smaller volcano that rose up from the floor of the harbour.

The local people have a story to explain this landform. The story says that a long time ago there was just one land mass. All the people lived harmoniously together on the land mass. They decided to have a great feast on the island of New Britain. All people attended. However, at the feast an argument and fight broke out.

The land was torn apart. The Beehives mark the spot where this happened.

The story and the science agree that once this area was all land. Now the sea has come in to create a harbour after several volcanic eruptions a long time ago. Powerful volcanoes have changed the shape of the land. Traditionally people came up with a different explanation. Both explanations tell us something of how people explain the past.

The Beehives

LANDFORMS AS SACRED PLACES

An entire landform or part of a landform may be a sacred place. Some islands are associated with special spirits and may be considered sacred. Many mountains are sacred places where spirits live. Mountains are important resources. People depend on them for water from streams; trees and plants like bamboo for building materials; animals and plants for food; and traditional medicine from bark, herbs and other plants.

Many places and special landforms were important in traditional beliefs. In Porgera, Enga Province, the hill that was a major source of gold ore for the mine was traditionally inhabited by a special sacred spirit. With the promise of benefits from the mine, people changed that knowledge or belief completely and were happy to sacrifice the spirit for the gold.

TRADITIONAL RESOURCES FROM LANDFORMS

Different landforms supply various traditional resources. Consider plains, for example. River plains are an important landform in Papua New Guinea. The Sepik plain provides fertile soil for gardening.

Soil is just one important resource found on the plain. Plentiful kunai grass is another resource. Traditionally, this grass is used in many ways. One important way is for the roofs for some types of traditional houses. Clan and family members harvest kunai grass to use in building a house. Men and women will have different roles

Kunai grass is traditionally used for roofing.

in this. In parts of the Sepik, the men do the building and the women prepare food for the house builders and transport the kunai grass to them.

EXPLORE

Compare the different examples given above with examples from your area or other parts of Papua New Guinea that you know about.

DEALING WITH NATURAL HAZARDS

Local communities needed to develop knowledge about natural hazards to survive. People who did not learn could be injured or die. Groups who forgot what had been learned were at risk.

You can explore local knowledge about natural hazards. You might start by asking people what the natural dangers of their area are. You might pick one hazard and then look for people from different areas to see how their community handles the hazard.

Below are a few examples of different types of hazards around Papua New Guinea and some of the traditional knowledge about them. You can collect more on these or others.

VOLCANOES

There are stories in the Highlands about the time of darkness. This was when volcanic ash covered large areas. The last major eruptions that carried ash to the Highlands were hundreds of years ago. Yet there are still stories of gardens dying and people dying if they went outside. The traditional wisdom is to stay indoors and save food. This is right because breathing ash can be deadly. The ash will also settle on plants and kill them, so saving food is important.

When Tavurvur started erupting in Rabaul in 1994, older people recognised the warning sign of pressure coming from beneath them. It was not like ordinary earthquakes rocking from side to side. Rather the earth movement seemed to come from directly below. They were able to warn others. This helped with the evacuation of villages and people in the city.

Some people have left Rabaul forever. Others are coming back. The traditional connection to the land is stronger than the volcanic hazard. The photograph on the next page shows how Rabaul is starting to re-green after volcanic eruptions that started in 1994.

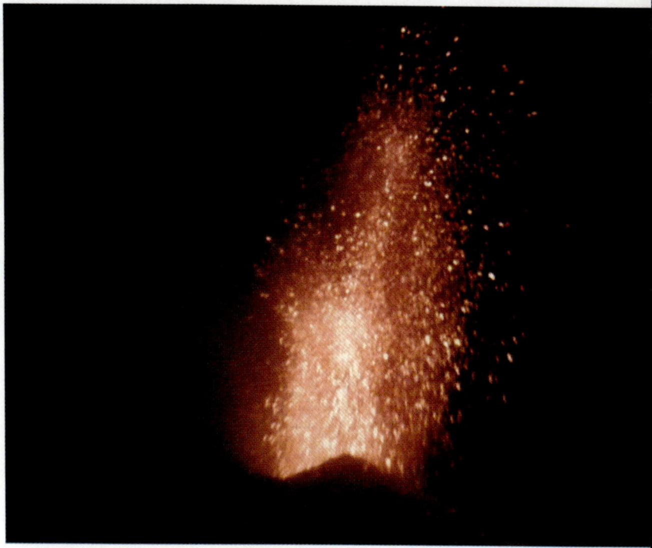

This photo shows Manam volcano erupting in 2012. This volcano is a hazard that the people live with on Manam Island. It is one of Papua New Guinea's most active volcanoes.

Here is Simpson Harbour with Tavurvur in the background. You can see how Rabaul is starting to re-green after volcanic eruptions that started in 1994.

Tavurvur continued erupting into 2010.
The coconuts are long dead, but the grasses and other greenery are starting to come back.

Traditionally people love their land and are starting to move back into Rabaul. Are they moving into a trap?

EXPLORE

What local knowledge can you find about volcanoes in your area?

WILD ANIMALS

Wild animals can be a natural hazard in most places of Papua New Guinea. Villagers may have many stories about different dangers from animals. These are a good starting point for learning about these hazards. Here are some examples.

Crocodiles

Crocodiles are a danger that people learn to live with. You remember the traditional stories about spirits in underwater canoes that attack people in the swamps? One type is a crocodile for sure!

You may be able to collect stories about crocodile attacks. There are traditional ways to avoid them and to survive. Traditional wisdom says that if a crocodile grabs you there are two ways to escape. For both ways, you must wait until you are in deep water.

- For the first way, you poke your thumb into the crocodile's eye as hard as you can. The crocodile should release you.
- The second way is if your arm is in the crocodile's mouth. You need to punch or poke into the throat. This breaks the seal and lets water in. The crocodile will drown if the seal stays open. Again you should be released. (But what if your arm is not long enough to reach the seal? Then attack the eyes.)

The crocodile is a natural hazard associated with special environments and landforms common in many parts of lowland Papua New Guinea.

Avoiding crocodile attack involves being careful on river banks, beaches and other places where crocodiles hunt. It means taking great care in swamps and other places, especially at night. Traditionally both Papua New Guineans and Africans will tell you to run in a zigzag if a crocodile is chasing you. This should help you escape. People know that if you run straight, it is easier for the croc to catch you.

Below are two true stories from people who survived a crocodile attack.

1 FROM EAST NEW BRITAIN

I am an East New Britain man. My friends and I went fishing in a big canoe one night. We caught plenty of fish and it was late. We came to the beach and decided to clean the fish at sunrise. We were so tired we slept on the beach.

I woke up when a crocodile grabbed me. He must have been hunting that night. Maybe he smelled the fish and found me. I knew the rules. Don't fight the crocodile on land. He can kill you. I pretended to be dead and waited. The crocodile took me and started to carry me out to sea. I knew a crocodile is helpless in deep water. As soon as the water deepened, I jammed my thumb into his eye. He spat me out. I swam back and my friends helped me. We never slept like that again. [This man had scars on his chest and back outlining a crocodile's teeth.]

2 FROM ORO PROVINCE

I live on the coast and was spearfishing next to a mangrove forest. The fishing was good. The tide was in and the water was fairly deep. It was about three o'clock in the afternoon. The next thing I knew, a big croc grabbed me and dove down. I never saw him sneak up on me.

I thought, 'Well, I am dead. I might as well see if these old stories are true about crocodile fighting.'

So I stuck my thumb as hard as I could into his eye. He stopped diving and swam straight up. His body came out of the water. He arched his back and threw me into the mangroves. I broke both legs landing on mangrove roots, but I survived.

Mangroves are rich sources of fish but can also be the location for dangerous crocodiles.

Pigs

Wild pigs are a food resource. They become a danger when wounded. A pig can kill by charging and ripping open the artery near a person's groin. If there are hunters in your area, you can explore the ways they try to protect themselves.

Because wild pigs are dangerous, catching them is a rite of passage in some places. It is a long and special process to prove manhood. In parts of Western Province, young men will catch a wild pig with just a cane rope. In parts of Gulf Province, young men will catch wild pigs with only their hands. In both cases, a natural hazard is being used for a traditional rite of passage to becoming a man.

Other animals

Snakes, wild dogs and centipedes are other examples of land animals that are natural hazards. Stonefish, sea urchins and sharks are all examples of creatures from the sea that are hazardous. You can collect information about these hazards and how people treat them. For a stonefish wound, as an example, both traditional and Western treatment is to use water as hot as possible on the wound. This helps stop the poison.

Stepping on a stonefish is one of the hazards of beaches and coral in Papua New Guinea. The sharp spines are poisonous and inflict a painful wound. There are traditional cures for this that work.

OTHER HAZARDS

Other common natural hazards include flood, drought, frost, tsunamis and landslips. See what local knowledge you can collect about these. Often the easiest way is to collect people's stories. See what lessons they teach you. The stories may stop you making mistakes with a hazard.

Below is one example about floods, from a man in Manus.

SURVIVING A FLOODED STREAM

When I was a small boy, my big brother and I went collecting in the bush. Our house was on a grassy slope. Below was a stream that we crossed. Then we walked across cleared land into the bush. We came home hours later.

In the meantime it had rained hard upstream. My mother saw us coming to the stream. It was in flood. It did not look dangerous to us. My mother shouted and waved. She was trying to warn us, but it was too late.

My brother picked me up and started crossing the stream. Then we found how powerful a flood current is. He could not stay on his feet. My mother was screaming and he managed to throw me to her. I was saved.

My brother was swept down the stream. He was a strong swimmer, but the water was much stronger. Luckily he got caught in tree branches and that saved him. He was badly cut and hurt, but he lived.

People teach traditional warnings in many places where they can see rain falling in the mountains and know that flooding in streams and rivers will follow. It is hard to understand just how strong water can be until you are swept along in such a flood.

EXPLORE

- What stories and knowledge can you find about hazards in your area? For example, is drought a hazard? What is the traditional solution? Or frost? Or something else?
- Share stories and see what general lessons you can learn from them.

DEBATE

Conduct a debate with two teams putting these different points of view:

- Team 1: Learning traditional ways to avoid or cope with natural hazards is very important.
- Team 2: We do not need local knowledge about hazards. The government or international aid will help us when we face a natural hazard.

CONNECTIONS BETWEEN THE LAND, VEGETATION AND CLIMATE

Traditional people all over Papua New Guinea understand how vegetation changes as you go higher up a mountain. Hunters know that the environments change and that different animals will be found in different environments determined by altitude.

All over PNG, people have long understood that vegetation changes with elevation and soil type.

Traditional people also understand that different vegetation may indicate different soils. In the Owen Stanley Mountains there are places where people still use slash-and-burn systems to grow crops. Villagers can pick out the best soil areas by the types of trees growing there. (They demonstrate an understanding of vegetation and the land.)

People have to know the right time to prepare and plant gardens. There is traditional knowledge about climate and the best times to make things grow. You can compare the type of climate you live in with the traditional knowledge about climate for your place.

When the leaves of the tropical almond or sea almond turn red, it is a sign used by some traditional coastal people that it is time to prepare their gardens for next year.

EXPLORE

Examine the rural areas around you and the most common traditional crops.

- How do people know when the best time to plant is?
- What are the traditional signs for planting?
- What are the traditional signs that it is time to start preparing gardens?
- Can you find links that show traditional knowledge understands the connections between the land, vegetation and local climate?
- How necessary is this knowledge for people making gardens in your area?

LAND USE

There are examples of traditional knowledge in land use all around Papua New Guinea. You can investigate any aspect you wish. Here are two ways to explore traditional land use:

1. Investigate practices and techniques that traditionally benefited the environment and helped people to maintain self-sufficiency. (This looks at parts of the system.)
2. Investigate traditional land use systems as they are working today under the impact of imported systems. Here you may find cases where tradition is used against the interests of some people in the community. (This looks at the whole system.)

Below are examples of these two ways to look at land use.

1 BENEFICIAL TECHNIQUES AND PRACTICES

Traditional ways to improve the soil for gardening

Soil is a very valuable resource. Farming people understand the need for good soil in order to have good crops. There is traditional knowledge about soil in each farming community. You can explore this knowledge.

In many traditional communities people will classify the soil. They know what soils are best for different crops. You may also find traditional ways people have protected or improved the soil.

Here are three traditional practices that help soil performance:

- Around Port Moresby, Motu gardeners use rock mulches in the dry season. They place rocks around food plants. The rocks help to hold moisture in the soil.
- In the Highlands people often use domestic pigs to dig up the soil for sweet potato mounds. The pigs help add air and waste matter to the soil. People may then add vegetable matter like dead vines, grasses and leaves buried in the mounds. This works as a soil enhancer.
- Traditionally people knew that the soil needed a rest or fallow period of 10 to 20 years. The bush regenerated and produced forest resources at the same time. This is an important technique to maintain and improve soils.

Traditional ways to reduce risk in the garden

Traditional gardeners and wise investors both limit their risks by spreading the possible gains. Good investors never put all their money in one investment. They will have four or five different investments. If one fails, there will still be money in the others. This is called 'spreading your bets'. It is also called 'diversifying your investments'.

Traditional gardeners used this principle long before money was invented. They understood the value of 'spreading your bets'. They would plant different crops in the same garden. If one failed or did poorly, there was still food available from the others.

Imported systems are monocultures. This means they plant one crop. If there is trouble, the whole crop suffers. You can ask people about rust fungus in coffee trees or die-back in cocoa trees.

You can compare how soil is treated today with past traditional practices. In parts of Papua New Guinea populations are much bigger. The old practices of shifting cultivation have changed. This puts more pressure on the soil. Crops are reduced or need fertiliser.

The food garden is one of the most important connections between land and people. The traditional garden was mixed. This is a coastal garden on Kitava Island. What foods can you see growing here? How wise is it to mix the crops in a garden?

Now look at this Highlands garden. What is similar to the traditional coastal garden? What is different? How are both these gardens different from imported agricultural systems?

MEN AND WOMEN'S KNOWLEDGE

Agriculture is the basis for traditional self-sufficiency. Different gardening tasks are often divided between male and female roles in PNG villages. This means knowledge may be divided between men and women. Often men will do the clearing, fencing and sometimes planting. Women will tend the gardens and do the weeding and harvesting.

EXPLORE

In your area, see what differences you can find in land use knowledge between men and women who have food gardens.

- What knowledge is important for people to successfully produce traditional foods?
- What knowledge do the women have?
- What knowledge do the men have?
- Is this changing?
- Are roles in gardening and raising animals changing?

2 CHANGES TO THE SYSTEMS AND THE RELATIONSHIP BETWEEN PEOPLE AND THE LAND

Now we look at the larger systems of tradition. These are changing. Below are two examples. One is from a patrilineal tradition and the other is matrilineal.

EXAMPLE 1: THE WAMPAR PEOPLE

The Wampar people live around the Markham and Wampit Rivers in Morobe Province. In the past, the land provided them with everything. It met their basic needs for food and shelter. The most important land use was gardening.

Traditionally this is a patrilineal society. The males of the landowning family or clan inherit land rights. This includes control over access to the land. The eldest male is the principal custodian to manage and share land. This person has both an obligation and a responsibility to do this. In the past, the elder ensured his people had access to land for food and other resources.

Although this society is patrilineal, females too are permitted the extended use of land in the traditional relationship between land and people.

Today there are many changes that alter the relationship of people to land. These changes include:

- a long period of contact with outsiders
- changes to leadership and government
- mining, cash crops and other new livelihood experiences
- the influence of education.

All these changes have had one major impact on land: the value of land has increased. Now it is often seen as a commodity for sale or rent. It has a money value.

In some places, these changes have weakened the traditional system and values of land associated with sharing and caring for the basic needs of food and shelter. But they have not weakened the tradition of ownership. Some male custodians of the customary

One reason land has become more valuable is because it can be used for the production of high-yielding cash crops such as cocoa, coffee and oil palm.

land have taken advantage of the traditional roles that give them land rights and control. They have used their position for their own gain. The land has become something to provide them with wealth, cash and social status. Many of the old obligations have been forgotten. The custodians have moved away from their traditional relationship to the land. They are now seen as having more imported business values.

Imported ideas about land and people have changed Wampar relationships. The eldest member of the family or kinship group has now acquired higher social status, associated in some cases with a monopoly over land rights and the control of access to land. This is a new interpretation of ownership. It means that the other male members of the family have use rights but little control over access to land.

Female family members retain use rights through marriage to local men, but they may lose these rights if they marry non-local men. For example, this happens if the woman marries a migrant man who has come to the village. Thus gender discrimination occurs with land access and use rights. A local woman in this category will have a low social status and be treated as an 'outsider'. Having a low status may mean that her household is only permitted limited land use rights for food production. They cannot produce cash crops as this is perceived to pose competition with landowners. Such households are often short of much-needed food and cash.

EXPLORE

Look at the traditional land rights and land use around you.

- Is cash making a difference to how land is viewed?
- Are some people losing part of their share to land access and use?
- How is tradition changing?
- Who is benefiting?
- Who is losing?

EXAMPLE 2: MUSSAU ISLAND

A special relationship exists between the people of Mussau Island in New Ireland Province and their land. People have traditionally lived and used land handed down through a family inheritance or accessed land through the fulfilment of social obligations, including funeral obligations. Land ownership is a symbol of individual, family and kinship identity and history because land is an inheritance from the ancestors.

Genealogies are associated with land ownership. In this matrilineal society, genealogies provide a family's evidence of shared roots and connections. A landowning family's rights have traditionally been obtained from kinship relations traced orally through a family tree. As a part of that story, oral evidence is provided about specific links between important ancestors and clan leaders. The evidence tells of the settlement and physical activities they conducted on the land over several generations. The evidence will also tell of those peoples with whom land access rights are to be shared.

Mussau Island is to the far north of the mainland. It is one of the important places where the Lapita people settled some 3500 years ago, before moving out to colonise the Pacific Islands. They took with them many traditionally used trees like breadfruit and plants like taro, as well as pigs, chickens and dogs. These first colonisers changed the landscapes and land uses of many islands across the Pacific.

Land was security for life. To be a landowner implied having food and material and environmental security. Traditionally land was used to:

- cultivate food crops
- hunt animals for food
- gather medicinal plants
- harvest marine and plant material
- provide building materials
- provide secure settlements that were safe during warfare.

These activities were interwoven with the people's culture involving rituals and emotional, moral and ethical values and practices. It was not uncommon for a fishing trip to be preceded by fasting, eating of specific foods only, or the gathering and use of special plant materials to make successful fish-catching. Land on which such traditional ancestral activities (including farming of special crops) were undertaken might be maintained with clearly established linkages between that land and its owners. Such was the social and sacred link between people and their land.

Today changes are seeping into the traditional relationships between land and people on Mussau Island. In the past, land rights were held by elderly female members of the lineage, but control of access was negotiated between elderly women and their elderly brothers or uncles. Men's major role was to guard and protect the land and their women and children.

To a certain extent, these practices are still happening. But today younger women may also be given stories about land. These stories explain land boundaries and rights, but access to land is sometimes a power struggle.

Younger men or women with an education, power or higher socio-economic status compete with the elderly women or men to assert both control of rights and access.

The introduction of cash into the economy appears to influence this. A good example is where cash crops start to generate income through changed land use. The changes give a person more cash. This raises their status and influence in the community. This can lead to tension. In recent times a couple of incidences of physical violence have occurred that have claimed a few lives.

Relationships between extended family members and other people in the community now depend a lot on the absence or presence of disputes over rights or access to land. People's desire for cash can conflict with the old ways of using the land. Good community relationships exist where there is no land dispute. Land is often at the base of bad relationships. The strength of family and people's identity and obligations to one another also are determined by commonly known rights and access to land.

Traditional culture derives from the land. Look at this dancer. The decoration or bilas *comes from plants, teeth, feathers, seeds, shells and other resources from the local environment. Everything is a part of the land. People have used products from their environment to create a dramatic art of body decoration. These decorations show people's close connection and interaction with the land. At the same time, this person is performing for cash. Can cash and tradition coexist harmoniously? With land, it has been very difficult so far.*

THE NEXT SEVEN CHAPTERS

We now move to other topics in the next seven chapters. In each one you will also see links to land use. Land remains a foundation for tradition.

CHAPTER 2

TRADITION AND PEOPLE ON THE MOVE

Unit 2 Grade 9 looks at how societies are growing, moving and changing. Growth, movement and change were parts of traditional societies too. Everywhere you look in your community, you will be able to find links between what you study in this unit and local knowledge.

The three major areas in this chapter are covered in the curriculum as 'population change', 'migration/population patterns' and 'the pull of the city'. Possibilities for exploring traditional and community knowledge within these include:

- traditional approaches to growing populations and their impacts on the land
- traditional practices taken to urban environments
- traditional links between rural and urban environments.

Much of what you look at in this chapter is based on traditional relationships. These are often not immediately visible. They are based on clan, family and culture (*kastom* or *pasin*). These invisible links are all around you. For example, perhaps you or some of your teachers are migrants. Students are one example of people moving for education. Teachers are one example of people moving for a job or income opportunity.

Migrant families may be split between different groups. People find themselves negotiating new traditional relationships. They also work to maintain traditional links and relationships.

TRADITIONAL APPROACHES TO GROWING POPULATIONS AND THEIR IMPACTS ON THE LAND

The evidence of the prehistory is clear. Papua New Guinea has long had slowly growing populations. People had to develop ways to deal with population growth. There were various traditional solutions to population pressure.

CONFLICT AND VIOLENCE

In the past, when populations grew too big, warfare was a common solution. People fought and killed for land. A stronger group could move in and take the land away from a weaker group. This could force some populations to retreat to poorer land or defensive settlements like ridge tops. For some, the result of warfare could be annihilation or forced migration. In other instances, the winners made slaves of the losers.

Two other violent responses to population pressure were cannibalism and infanticide. They belong to the past. They are good examples of traditions no longer practised or desired. An alternative to violence is cooperation and intensification.

IMPROVING FOOD PRODUCTION

There are more people to feed when populations grow. One solution is to produce more food. People invent more productive agricultural systems or ways to exploit the environment. This requires cooperation. People have had to get on together to create some of the larger traditional agricultural systems of PNG.

Traditionally, the Highlands had increasingly dense populations. Lowland populations may have suffered from the introduction of malaria thousands of years ago. But both Highlands and lowlands show processes of agricultural intensification over time. Now new crops are being added alongside traditional ones.

Papua New Guinea has many examples of people making their land more productive. Hunter-gatherer people may have turned to forest management as an early example. They may have cleared around pandanus trees and protected other food trees. These practices could help slowly growing populations.

Agricultural systems became more intensive with growing populations. You can see this in the horticulture of the Highlands. Growing populations started using the land more intensively. The first evidence is at Kuk in Western Highlands Province. The systems for growing taro and bananas there have become more intensive over thousands of years.

Today you see the most intensive land use where rural populations are largest. The sweet potato has replaced earlier staple crops in the Highlands. It is intensively grown using various systems to maintain soil fertility. In areas of much lower population, there was traditionally much less intensive agriculture. This general pattern can still be seen.

LABOUR SHARING

Giving everyone a chance to work on food production was another traditional way to help distribute food in a growing population. Below is a description of traditional labour sharing in Tasitel Village on Mussau Island.

LABOUR SHARING ON MUSSAU ISLAND

Islands have limited good land. What happens as populations grow? Differences in access to good garden land emerge over time. On Mussau Island, good garden land was unequally distributed. One traditional way to meet this population pressure peacefully was through labour sharing. Here is how it worked in one village.

Those landowners with plenty of good land invited the have-nots or friends to cultivate taro on allocated portions of gardening land. Community folk were invited to assist with clearing the gardening land and those who assisted were likely to receive an allocation of land. Thus labour sharing guaranteed access to gardening land that was farmed for years.

The tradition carried obligations. When you gardened on someone else's land, the harvest of the first crops was given to the landowner. This was a thank you and showed respect to the landowners.

This system worked well with the village population size and density prior to the 1980s. Since then, continuing population increase in the village has put pressure on the demand and need for access to land for gardening and houses and even for income-generating activities.

Today, traditional land rights and claims are often challenged. Descendants of farmers have challenged landowners' rights due to ignorance of original land tenure arrangements. It appears that increasing populations have brought about this scenario. Sometimes landowners have to publicly defend their claims, with elders called as witnesses to verify oral accounts over land claims.

Population pressure is starting to raise conflicts over traditional land use and land rights. Some people are simply leaving. People going to the courts and migrating are two solutions today. The court system is imported. The migration solution links to past behaviours.

Often land disputes and deliberations today are settled in village courts.

MIGRATION

Another traditional solution to population pressure has been migration. People searched for unoccupied land and moved there. This process resulted in the settling of the Highlands as well as the far Pacific Islands. In some cases migration led to warfare when people took over other people's land. Sometimes the losers also moved to poorer resource areas and then adapted to use that land.

Everywhere in the Highlands you will find influences of migration between many different areas. Look at this picture and see what traditional knowledge is visible and what imported knowledge is also visible.

Traditionally people moved from place to place in many parts of Papua New Guinea. The most common form of migration was moving from one garden area to another. Slash-and-burn systems of agriculture had people moving in ten- and twenty-year cycles to allow soils to replenish. Population pressure limited many of these traditional systems.

Traditionally, some people had to move when populations became too large. For example, look at Chimbu today. You will find village people with claims to land far from where they live. Some claims are based on marriage. Some claims are based on battles fought long ago. They all point to the many different interactions between land and people in the past. They also provide examples of traditional approaches to growing populations and the impact these had on the land.

TRADITIONAL PRACTICES TAKEN TO URBAN ENVIRONMENTS

The city is an imported concept in Papua New Guinea. But a look at any city in the country will show traditional knowledge being brought to the urban environment. Here are some examples. You should be able to find many more traditional practices taken to urban environments.

USING THE TRADITIONAL KINSHIP OR *WANTOK* NETWORK FOR SUPPORT

Unemployed migrants in urban environments use a number of traditional practices and customs for survival.

First, contrary to the nuclear households of urban environments in the West, the first and strongest traditional practice in PNG's urban centres is in family structure. The strength of the kinship network or extended family is the source of social and economic support for migrants. Even settlement dwellings are oriented and arranged by ethnic group and family.

Because of the high costs of urban living, jobless migrants will transit indefinitely with relatives in an urban residence. Their ultimate aim, however, is to settle in a peri-urban destination of settlements, squatter settlements or blocks. ('Peri-urban' means on the edge or perimeter of the urban area.)

LABOUR SHARING IN THE URBAN ENVIRONMENT

Labour sharing is another traditional practice that migrants have taken to urban environments. Here migrants assist *wantok* residents with their livelihood creation, maintenance or income generation. In this way migrants derive food, accommodation and security from working and helping. This process may take years until they find an income-generating activity of their own.

GROWING TRADITIONAL CROPS

Many migrants on the edge of urban areas cultivate traditional food crops such as sweet potato, corn, peanuts and bananas, despite the low cash returns from their sales.

MAINTAINING TRADITIONAL CUSTOMS

Migrants continue to practise many traditional customs and ceremonies. These can include mutual exchanges of cash, pigs and wealth. These customs are practised in cities and towns and along their fringes where migrants settle. Traditional events include those for compensations, deaths, marriages, initiations and festive occasions.

These practices are built around the traditional concepts of obligation and kinship relationships. They provide people with their ancestral history and a sense of belonging. Though they have been modified by the introduction of cash, wealth and power, these practices continue to define the traditions of different communities.

MIGRANTS USING TRADITIONS TO RAISE CASH

Traditional arts are now a way to earn cash. These skills can be brought to urban locations by migrants. For example, there are large communities of Sepik carvers in Madang and Port Moresby. There are many other expressions of traditional art that are now worth money.

Migrants may find their traditions are worth money. Tourism is one area where migrants can earn money from traditional performances. Here are some men from Fergusson Island who have migrated to Alotau in Milne Bay. The migrants are performing for passengers on a cruise ship. At other times they may perform in hotels.

Mathias Kauage was a famous artist of Papua New Guinea. He came from Chimbu and migrated to Port Moresby. Here his wife and son show a picture the wife made to tell about her husband's life. Like many male migrants, Mathias Kauage worked on a coffee plantation before coming to Port Moresby. He used art to combine traditional and imported knowledge and skills. His wife, sons and other migrants continue to use art as a way to earn cash and to leave some record of traditional knowledge.

DEBATE

Conduct a debate with two teams putting these different points of view:

- Team 1: Tourism can help people maintain and take pride in parts of their culture.
- Team 2: Tourism is another agent of change that weakens traditional culture.

In the complex world of today none of the above happens in isolation. You will see the mix everywhere of imported and traditional as you study the links between rural and urban environments.

Clans in New Ireland are divided into two large groups or moieties. One is called 'big' and the other 'little'. They are associated with the sea eagle and the fish hawk (in Tok Pisin, bikpisin *and* liklik pisin*). You see one symbol now drawn and written on laplaps sold in Kavieng. What does this mean for this ancient tradition and its urban connection? (The other symbol is a* nilpis.*)*

LANGUAGE AND MIGRATION

Language is a good example of traditional knowledge taken to urban environments.

Language is an important part of tradition. Around the world, many languages are disappearing. Some traditions will disappear when a language is lost. At the same time, new languages may take some of the lost language's traditions. A new language may start new traditions.

Language is often an important part of migration. This is true for rural-to-urban migration, rural-to-rural migration and migration to mining or other enclaves. People who migrate often must learn a new language. Also, migrants will bring their language with them.

DISCUSS

You have heard the Tok Pisin word *wantok* many times. Now think about it:

- Where does the word *wantok* come from?
- What does it tell you about migration?
- What does it tell you about migrants?
- How could you link a study of *wantoks* to history?
- What other chapters in this book could you link ideas about *wantoks* to?

Tok Pisin made by migrants

Tok Pisin is a language developed by Melanesians. It was made by labour or work migrants. Plantation workers made this language from their own languages, English, German and Malay. It is a new tradition for communicating. You can find many interesting ways of expressing ideas in it. You can also watch it change as new words come into it.

Tok Pisin is used to communicate ideas within the community.

For example, migrants use Tok Pisin to express their livelihood and lifestyle, their community status and their identity. Look at these words:

Kam manmeri. This is what migrants call themselves. They use *kam manmeri* to refer to themselves as migrant males and females who were not born in their usual place of residence.

Fri fud or *free food* is food produced directly from the garden. The term can also mean access to land, even customary land, for residence and gardens. Migrants to urban places who do not find regular incomes are often concerned with *fri fud*.

Hevi refers to important life events that now need cash. These include traditions such as initiations, bride price ceremonies, marriages, compensation ceremonies and ceremonies for deaths. Parts of these traditions are now cash-based. They require large amounts of money to be done properly. They are a *hevi* or a burden. Migrants may have to return home or complete other traditional obligations. You see that tradition is still very important to family members and sponsors with an added burden of finding cash.

Seves or *service* is a word that means assistance, aid or self-help. *Seves* helps migrant households to meet their basic needs for things like shelter, food and security. *Seves* can be any form of self-help or assistance. It includes:

- cash-earning opportunities
- cash loans
- cash crop activities like raising poultry or growing coffee, cocoa or betel nut
- wage employment

- street and market sales
- other self-employment
- church, government or non-government projects and programs.

EXPLORE

- What other words can you find with meanings developed by migrants?
- What do these new meanings tell us about the migrant experience?
- How do they help us understand this experience?
- How do they show links between migrants and their original homes?

DEBATE

Conduct a debate with two teams putting these different points of view:

- Team 1: Cash is changing migrant lives completely and changing traditions to something very new.
- Team 2: Cash is the means migrants now use to keep many traditions alive, with tradition only changing slowly.

Migrants may speak several languages

All over Papua New Guinea, people are moving. They are looking for jobs, education, health services and new opportunities. They bring languages with them. Different languages are an important part of migration, linking with traditions. Being able to speak different languages can also be considered an important human resource.

THE LANGUAGE ADVANTAGE

Science has shown that learning two languages helps the brain to develop. A person who learns two languages by the time they are four years old will have a different brain from a person who only learns one language. Many Papua New Guineans will speak two languages before the age of four. This makes it easier for them to learn other languages later in life.

A person who speaks two languages is called *bilingual*. Many Papua New Guineans speak more than two languages. Some are trilingual (speak three languages) or multilingual (speak a number of languages). How many languages can you speak?

Here is a boat of people going to Madang from a settlement. It is early morning. They go to work or earn money or study. How many different languages do you think the people on this boat might speak?

DISCUSS

- How valuable is it to be able to speak two or more languages? What type of human resource is this?
- How valuable is it to be able to learn languages easily?
- What is the language situation in your area?
- How important are *tok ples*, Tok Pisin and English?

EXPLORE

You can explore how different languages bring different ideas with them.

- You can compare different PNG languages with Tok Pisin and English. Use your knowledge of traditional languages. Check your own knowledge with that of other speakers of that language. If you speak no traditional language, seek help from people who do speak a traditional language.
- You can make a table or chart to compare and contrast. Below is one way to do it.

COMPARE AND CONTRAST ANOTHER LANGUAGE(S) WITH TOK PISIN AND ENGLISH

Greetings: How do you say hello? How do you greet people in different situations?	
XX language	Find examples from your experience and/or from other people who speak the language. Do older people remember different ways used in the past that are gone now?
XXY language	You may wish to have more than one traditional language to compare.
Tok Pisin	For example: *Moning* or *moning tru*, *apinun* or *apinun tru* are commonly used at different times of the day. May also use *gude* or *halo*. May mention number of persons and gender, for example, *Moning tru tripela meri or Apinun tru tupela pikinini.* You can continue with other greetings you know of.
English	'Hello' and 'good day' are commonly used. 'Good morning', 'good afternoon' and 'good evening' are also used for different times of the day. You can continue with more information.
Farewells: How do you say goodbye? How do you farewell people in different situations?	
XX language	As above, find examples from your experience and/or from other people who speak the language. Do older people remember different ways used in the past that are gone now?
XXY language	You may wish to have more than one traditional language to compare.
Tok Pisin	For example: *Lukim yu* or *lukum yu narapela taim* are commonly used. May also use *gutbai.* You can continue with other farewells you know of.
English	'Goodbye' is often more formal. 'See you' or 'see you later' are less formal. Other terms include 'catch you later', 'so long' or 'take care'. You can continue with more information.

Wise sayings and advice: What wise sayings and common advice appear in this language?	
XX language	Find examples from your experience and/or from other people who speak the language. Do older people remember different ways used in the past that are gone now?
XXY language	You may wish to have more than one traditional language to compare.
Tok Pisin	For example: *Maski wori* or *maski wori em samting nating* (don't worry about it, it is nothing). You can continue with other wise sayings you know of.
English	Parents often say 'Be good' to children or young adults; friends may say this to each other. 'A stitch in time saves nine' means it is better to maintain something than to let it break and then have to fix it. You can continue with more information.
Numbers: What numbers and number systems appear in this language? You may ask your maths teacher for help on systems and terms.	
XX language	Find examples from your experience and/or from other people who speak the language. Do older people remember different ways used in the past that are gone now?
XXY language	You may wish to have more than one traditional language to compare.
Tok Pisin	Two types of numbering. The first is abstract: *wan, tu, tri* and so on. The second is concrete: *wanpela, tupela, tripela* and so on. You can continue with other numbers and number uses you know of.
English	English commonly uses the decimal system. A much older tradition is the system of Roman numerals: I, II, III, IV, V and so on. (The Roman system is still used by movie makers to make it harder to work out how old a film is.) You can continue with more information.

You may continue with as many other comparisons and contrasts as you wish, for example:

- **Pronouns:** What are the terms for I, you, we, them, me and us?
- **Family members:** What terms are used for family members? Are there terms for special friends?
- **Special life events:** What terms are used for birth, initiation, weddings and funerals?
- **Categories:** What different types of categories are there? For example, 'flying things' may include all things that fly. This puts birds, insects, gliders and bats all in the same category. English is different. Think of the category of 'mammals', which only includes animals that feed their young with milk; a few fly but most do not.
- Write a conclusion when you finish your comparisons. Tell what differences you see between the languages. What does this tell you about tradition, values and roles in Papua New Guinea? What does it tell you about a possible resource that migrants have?

TRADITIONAL LINKS BETWEEN RURAL AND URBAN ENVIRONMENTS

There are many traditional links or connections between urban and rural populations through migration. One of the strongest is maintaining traditional land rights when a migrant is away. People will maintain contact and support between rural and urban areas. *Wantoks* use each other for visits that can be both social and economic.

EXPLORE

Explore the use of traditional links in your area. It does not matter if it is rural or urban. You are looking at the connections between the two:

- What traditional links can you find with migrants to or from your area?
- What traditions do migrants help maintain?
- What traditions do you think are being lost?
- Do you think migration is strengthening, weakening or starting new traditions in your area?

You will see that traditional links between rural and urban environments are strong. These links exist and are supported in several interrelated ways. Links include the following:

- Migration of people between rural and urban areas creates a social, tradition-based link between those in rural areas and those in urban areas. Sometimes these relations may be weak. Usually they are strong. They often involve traditional economic reciprocity. These relationships may be reinforced by mutual visits to and from rural/urban areas. This includes the exchange of goods and items.
- Residents of urban areas may sponsor members of their extended family to come and live in the urban area. Sometimes new migrants come uninvited but are still supported based on traditional values.
- Imported communication linkages are growing for the transfer of messages and information between rural and urban areas. This stimulates both social and economic interaction. Again, it can work to strengthen traditional interaction. Using traditional languages with imported communication systems is a key way of keeping traditional links between rural and urban environments.
- The flow of goods and services between urban and rural areas links these environments. Some of these goods and services are based on traditional knowledge and ideas.

Imported transportation systems on land, sea, air and road make the movement of people between rural and urban areas much easier. The imported systems provide accessible and affordable transport. This in turn supports the movement of traditional knowledge and ideas.

This looks like a traditional Sepik village, but look closely. What links to the city can you see? What links can't you see, but suspect are there too?

MAKING MORE CONNECTIONS

STRETCH YOUR THINKING

There are many other ways to consider the links between traditional knowledge and population changes. The next section looks at a very difficult area. This is sorcery. It affects all Papua New Guineans.

You could study it in Unit 3 Grade 9 (on History), Unit 4 Grade 9 (on Civics) or Unit 3 Grade 10 (on conflict). You may want to come back to it then or use it now.

This is just one example of how parts of traditional knowledge can link into many of your school studies if you stretch your thinking to make connections.

SORCERY: A TRADITION THAT PUSHES PEOPLE TO MIGRATE

Growing populations may not have enough land. This leads to conflict. Some of the growing problems with sorcery may be tied to the interaction between land and people. Sorcery or the accusation of sorcery becomes one traditional approach to a growing population. Fear of sorcery can lead people to migrate a long way from their village of origin.

Sorcery is a troubling part of traditional knowledge. It raises questions about what is valuable from the past and what is dangerous from the past.

How sorcerers work

Sorcery uses various elements to gain power over people. Sorcerers can use magical thinking to make people believe that the sorcerer has power. The belief gives the sorcerer power in their minds.

Magical thinking is based on creating connections. The two most common connections are:

1. Connections between things that seem to be alike in some way. A magic stone may look like a face, for example. A magic stick may look like a snake. Another type of connection is to name an animal the same name as an enemy and then kill the animal.
2. Connections between things that have once actually been together. A very common type of magic is to take some part of a person, such as hair or toenails they have cut and left. The sorcerer claims a connection to the person through these parts.

Another common example is taking a fresh-picked leaf and placing it on your property. Your touching the leaf connects it to you and protects the property even if you are not there.

Connecting things that happen one after another is also common among sorcerers. This is a false type of reasoning (sometimes called a *post hoc* error). Just because something happens after something else does not mean the first thing made it happen. For example, singing every morning to make the sun come up is a *post hoc* error. You may think your singing is making the sun come up, but it really does nothing.

Putting stones in water to make it rain may have started as a *post hoc* error. Putting stones in water for rain is an example of magical thinking that connects two things, water and rain, because they are similar. Someone may have thought, 'If I put magic stones in water, this will bring rain.' The stones went in and it rained, but it was not really the stones that did it.

Sorcery is more than just using the mind to gain power over people. Sorcery can use deadly poisons made from plants, animals and human waste. These are not magic. They are poison just like insecticides and herbicides. Both of these imported poisons have been linked to sorcery practices.

The power of suggestion

Sorcery uses the power of suggestion to make a person feel unwell. For more than 100 years, scientists have recorded how strong the power of suggestion is. It can result in whole groups of people feeling sick just from the panic of *thinking* they are sick.

The power of suggestion can be used when a sorcerer points a crystal at someone and then cracks a dry stick. The person knows they have been sorcered by the crystal. The suggestion is powerful and can make them sick.

The placebo effect

The opposite of this is the placebo effect. A placebo is something in medicine that has no power in itself. There are many different placebo effects. A pretend operation is one example. Another common example is giving people sugar pills and telling them that these pills will stop pain. This works for some people. This effect can be used by sorcerers to counter someone who thinks they have been cursed.

You should know that the placebo effect is real. That is, scientists have measured changes in people using placebos. Similarly, scientists have measured real changes in people suffering from fear and stress. Stress can kill people. This includes stress caused by fear that a person is being sorcered.

Fear

Fear is the most powerful tool of sorcery. Fear is a powerful human emotion. It is important for survival; you need fear to stop you from doing things that could harm or kill you. Some fear is normal and all people experience some fear.

The misuse or manipulation of fear is the problem. It can easily lead people to panic. Fear and panic cause people to act in ways that are poorly thought out. They may lead to migration to escape a threat. They may lead to fighting. They may lead to mobs turning on people suspected of sorcery and killing them.

Fear can be used as a weapon to control people and gain power. Sorcerers, dictators, terrorists and manipulative politicians are all people who use fear to get or keep power.

EXPLORE

Discuss the practice and fear of sorcery in your area as it links to migration into or out of a community:

- Can you find any examples in your community or in a community you know about where the fear of sorcery has made people migrate somewhere else?
- Can you find any examples in your community or in a community you know about where the fear of sorcery is keeping different clans or other groups apart?
- Does fear of sorcery keep different migrant groups apart?
- What ways can you find to protect people against sorcery?

TRADITIONAL KNOWLEDGE OF THE PAST

Unit 3 Grade 9 explores the history of Papua New Guinea. You may investigate some part of the history of your local area. You may study almost any area of traditional knowledge from the distant past to the present.

Here are some examples of how you can explore parts of Melanesian history. There are clues all around. You just need to follow them up to see what they can tell you about the past.

THE SING SING

Every time you see people dressed for a sing sing you are looking at an ancient tradition. But it is one that keeps changing. The photographs on the next page give some evidence for you to consider.

DISCUSS

- What is similar between the rock art and the shadows of the sing sing dancers on the following page?
- What does this suggest about the history of sing sing ceremonies?
- How would the shadow of a sing sing dancer from your area compare with these pictures?

SING SINGS—A HISTORY OF CHANGE

Sing sings are a very visible part of tradition. You can explore the history of sing sings in your area. You will be looking at a part of Melanesian tradition that goes back for thousands of years. It is still adapting and changing with the times.

Traditionally, one reason for sing sings was to provide a way for young men and women to get together. Another reason was to bring villagers together for a feast and peaceful time. In many parts of Papua New Guinea this has now changed. So there is a history to the changes in these traditions.

This painting shows human figures. They seem to be dancing. This is rock art from the Kimberley in north-west Australia. It is some of the oldest art in the world. No one is sure if it is 40 000 or 20 000 years old, but it is very old. No one is sure who the artists were or what happened to them, but they left thousands and thousands of rock paintings. They lived in this area when New Guinea and Australia were all one land mass and left the area maybe 8000 years ago when the New Guinea and Australian lands were separated by the sea. That is all that is known about them.

Here are dancers for a sing sing in Madang province. Look at the shadows they make. Compare the shadows with the ancient rock art from the Kimberley region of Australia.

DISCUSS

You can explore what changes have taken place in sing sings through questions like these:

- Are there still traditional reasons for sing sings in your area?
- What newer reasons can you find for sing sings today?
- Why did people do sing sings in the past?
- What memories are there of these?
- How can you document the changes to sing sings for your community group?
- What is the history of the sing sing for your people?
- Consider the decorations people use. Are they changing? What is different now? What did the different decorations mean? What are the reasons for them now?
- What musical instruments are used at local sing sings? Can you find stories about their history?
- What do the songs or chants mean? Can they tell you anything about the history of the sing sing?
- How important has cash become to sing sing performances?

Trobriand school students perform in a sing sing. They enjoy doing traditional Trobriand dances and like to try other traditions. For example, the boys will also do dances from Manus. This sing sing is helping to raise money for community services. Already you can start to see a history of changes to traditions.

In Watam Village, East Sepik Province, the water spirit comes out of a special place where only men are allowed. The spirit moves rhythmically through the village. It is a more specialised ceremony with similarities to the sing sing. In many places, people have stopped these specialised ceremonies. Can you find any trace or history of special ceremonies in your area?

OTHER HISTORIES OF TRADITIONAL CHANGE

You can do similar histories of change for other traditional activities and knowledge. Analyse how they have changed over time. This type of study can record a part of your own local history.

HISTORY OF WOMEN

Women do much of the food production and early child rearing in Papua New Guinea. Without food and children there would be no foundation to traditional life. Often women are forgotten in history.

You may wish to explore the history of some of the women around you. You could start with your mother and a grandmother or other older woman. You might want to compare the experiences and histories of women from different places. One could be a migrant history, the other a history of a woman who did not have to move.

EXPLORE

You could explore questions like these:

- What has happened in their life? What is their history?
- What changes have they seen in Papua New Guinea?
- How different was their childhood from yours?
- How have the roles of women changed?
- What are the most important things a mother needs to teach her children?
- How different is it for boys and girls now from when she was a child?

Mothers and daughters do much of the hard work to produce food and raise families in rural Papua New Guinea. How far back can you take their histories? See what information you can find from women around you.

STORIES OF LONG AGO

There are many stories from the past. Each area of Papua New Guinea is filled with stories that may explain parts of the past. Any time you record one of these stories you are preserving some small part of history.

You can search for stories that explain the past. Some old people may have stories that are being lost. Here is an example from two brothers, Peter Furebi and Fanwell Bedada of Kasiawa, Cape Nelson. (I spoke to them and recorded this in 1979.) They were part of a very small group of people who still spoke Kerebi, an Austronesian language. The Kerebi people have now been displaced and absorbed by non-Austronesian speakers. (The Korafe people absorbed the Kerebi and most of their land long ago.)

STORIES OF THE KEREBI PEOPLE'S PAST

'The Kerebi people were always here. In the distant past there was no light. All was darkness. The Kerebi people had to do everything with fire for light—gardening, hunting and fishing. They had no houses and lived in the kunai grass, in caves and around large rocks.

'At the same time, a large black bush pheasant lived in their area. He is still found in the kunai grass today. This bird lived in a house. One day the Kerebi people decided to attack the bush pheasant. The men chased the bird away and saw his house. They discovered the plan for the house and that is how they build houses today.

'In the Korafe language, the bird is called *siao*. This comes from the longer name in Kerebi, which is *mamu wabina siao anabare*.

The scientific name for this bird is Violaceous coucal. *It lives in many parts of Papua New Guinea and has a nest of leaves and twigs found in deep kunai. Are there stories about this bird in your area? Or stories about other birds?*

'The Kerebi people built their house but they still lived in darkness and needed light. The women used to see a small light out in the direction of Goodenough Island. It was just a little light, and every time they worked in the gardens they could see it. So the women told their husbands to find out what it was.

'One day all the men got in a very big canoe to find out about the light. When they got to where the light was, they discovered an old lady with a bamboo pipe (for smoking). The light was inside the pipe. This old lady used to set the pipe in front of her and make bilums. The first time the men went across to see, she was making a bilum, so they could not get the pipe. They went across another time and she was asleep. The light in the pipe was still shining so the men went up and got it.

'Suddenly she woke up and looked for her bamboo. Then she said, *"Mena au mara?"* which means, "Where is my light?"

'The men ran down to the canoes with the bamboo. They started paddling back home. The old lady came running down to the sea after them, chasing them. When she came to the beach, she yelled, *"Waga! Waga!"* meaning, "Canoe! Canoe!"

'She followed the men and kept reaching out, nearly grabbing the bamboo. But each time the men pulled it away and paddled faster. She came after them, attacking them and making their escape harder and harder. One man was frightened and called out, "Give her back the bamboo", but they didn't do it. The old lady was still attacking them when they reached Kofure Point [on the coast of their land]. So one man smashed the bamboo open against the side of the canoe.

'When the bamboo broke, the daylight came. The sun started rising from Kofure Point, and that is why people thought the sun rose from Kofure Point. The Kerebi people then started living with light. Before, people used the coconut fronds to make fire for light. With the new light everyone was happy. They made feasts and celebrated.'

ANALYSE THE STORY FOR AN IDEA OF HISTORY

As you collect stories, you can analyse them to see what they tell you about the past. For example, in the Kerebi stories above:

- What do they tell you about what people did in the past?
- How did people relate to birds (and other animals) in their environment? What did they know about them?
- What types of technologies and resources are needed to make a big canoe that can travel long distances?
- What do they tell you about relationships between men and women in the past?
- What else does the story tell you about the past? Do you think the story might have changed over time? (For example, the lady had a bamboo pipe for smoking, but bush tobacco [*brus*] comes from the Americas and has probably been in PNG for only a few hundred years.) What might this tell you about these types of stories?

- How does this story compare with stories you can find in your area about people building houses or about the start of daylight? What other explanations can you find for the start of daylight?

Stories from the past may observe something in the environment. The storyteller uses the observation to try to explain something about people. In the Kerebi story, people observed the black pheasant and its nest. This may have been a *Violaceous Coucal*. Someone looked at the nest and thought, 'So this is how we learned about houses.'

You may find other examples of this process. For example, people wanted to explain death. There are various stories in Melanesia using observations from the environment to explain death. One theme is that snakes and people both used to live forever. When they got old they shed their skins. That made them young again. But then people lost the ability for one reason or another.

What this shows you is that people have long been using observation to reason. These stories and traditions are all part of people developing reasoning skills.

PRAISE, BLAME AND OTHER HUMAN VALUES TO EXPLAIN THE ENVIRONMENT

The tropical or sea almond tree is called *kariking* in Tok Pisin. The people on the Rai coast have a story for why the delicious kernel is so hard to get. They say that a long time ago it was easy to split open the fruit. Then a man made the spirit of the *kariking* tree angry. She made the kernel much harder to get, covering it with a very tough nut.

A kariking tree

EXPLORE

- Can you find other stories where people are blamed for making something become harder to do or to get?
- Can you find stories where people are praised for providing something? For example, there are stories about men turning into yams so their families could have something to eat. Is there any similar story for that or other food in your area?
- When you think about the history of people, what do these stories tell you?

STRETCH YOUR THINKING

A collection of local stories can help you with ideas about the community's history. It can help you infer what happened in the past. To *infer* means to use reasoning to come to a conclusion. The evidence the stories present allows you to reason or analyse what they may be telling you about the past. You can draw inferences about how they lived and what was important in past society.

THE START OF NEW TRADITIONS FROM THE PAST

You may be able to find bits of physical evidence about the start of new traditions in your area. Look at the photographs below. What history do they record? What do they tell you about the introduction of new traditions?

Here is a record of local history. It also tells about new traditions brought to Tami Island. You may find something similar in your area. You can then search and question to find out what happened and how it changed traditional knowledge.

Here is another historical record that started new traditions that combined with old ones. Again, it is an example of a starting point for your search about the history of traditional knowledge and how it has changed.

EXPLORE

How have various traditions combined in your area? For example, are there feasting and sing sings at Christmas? How does this combine tradition?

OTHER HISTORY TOPICS CONCERNING TRADITIONAL KNOWLEDGE

You can search for the history of any topic in this book. All the other chapters will give you some information about the past. They all provide ideas. You can use any of them to start a history study.

TRADITIONAL LEADERSHIP AND CIVICS

Unit 4 Grade 9, 'Civics and Citizenship', looks at how government works and how it *should* work. The main areas for looking at traditional knowledge apply to traditional leadership. You might investigate:

- How did traditional leadership work in the past? How does this influence the present?
- What were traditional ethics or values for leaders and followers? How important are traditional leadership values now? Do they help or stop PNG being a strong nation?

Traditional values for leaders and followers are woven together like strings in a bilum. Traditional leaders worked with traditional values or ethics. These values included ideas about give and take. They included land as the most valuable thing a group had. One part of the ethics or values dealt with who could use the land, for how long and what they had to share from the land. This included sharing from gardens and from the bush, which provided plants, animals and some minerals.

WHAT DID A TRADITIONAL LEADER DO?

First, ask yourself, 'What did a traditional leader do?' Across Papua New Guinea there were various types of leaders. They reflected various values. Each society had ideas about what a good or bad leader was. Most importantly, a good leader was one who ensured the group's survival.

Both men and women had leadership roles. Men stood out. Women tended to be in the background. This remains the case today. Men tend to be freer to speak out. They tend to push themselves forward. Women often do not speak up. They tend to feel reluctant to speak and may defer to men. This is changing, but it reflects the past.

Much traditional leadership is based on maintaining land ownership. Where men own the land, women are in a much weaker leadership position. Where women

A good traditional leader took care to see that everyone in the group got their fair share of access to land. This was at the base of traditional society. A fight leader protected the land from enemies and took land from enemies.

are the traditional landowners, the female owner's brother traditionally speaks for her, but she makes leadership decisions.

FOLLOWERS AND LEADERS

Traditional followers can be compared to citizens today. The traditional follower was loyal to the group and to its leader or leaders. Survival often depended on giving and paying back at different ceremonies and different times. People depended on each other to survive. These give-and-take relationships are called *reciprocal*. Reciprocity means paying back for something that is given.

This included human life. *Pay back* is often a term used only for human life. In fact, it is a base of tradition. Good leaders ensured that their groups could pay back at feasts and other ceremonies. All the followers understood these rules.

Good leaders managed claims for land and land use. Traditional leaders, both men and women, knew the group boundaries. They knew what land belonged to whom. They agreed on usage and ownership. Today Papua New Guineans are torn between imported systems of land ownership and traditional systems. Some leaders now only look after themselves and close family.

Resources have changed for leaders. Traditional leaders had power over land and land use based on group ownership. The resources available to traditional leaders included pigs, shell

Symbols of leadership and importance in traditional systems are now losing the importance they once had. They may become items for sale for cash.

money or other prestige items, and feasting. Today cash has replaced many traditional resources for leaders. Big companies and overseas business people are able to provide cash. Leaders can use this to help keep them in power.

At the same time, followers demand gifts from leaders for their vote. The traditional system of give and take has slipped into voting. Leaders come under pressure to get votes. They may give away land rights and employment to overseas interests.

DISCUSS

- What parts of traditional leadership are good for us now?
- What parts of traditional leadership hurt us now?

DEBATE

Conduct a debate with two teams putting these different points of view:

- Team 1: We should leave tradition out of leadership and only follow an overseas model of democracy.
- Team 2: We can still have traditional leadership in government and develop a society that is fair to all.

LEADERSHIP IN DIFFERENT SOCIETIES

There are two basic traditional societies in Papua New Guinea: patrilineal and matrilineal. On the next page is an example of each.

- In the first one, former Chief Ombudsman Ila Geno answers questions about traditional leadership and provides information about how patriarchal leadership operated at the Hood Lagoon, Central Province.
- In the second one, Dr Jennifer Litau provides information about matriarchal leaders in Mussau Island, New Ireland. Both examples look at what you can learn from this type of leadership.

1 TRADITIONAL LEADERSHIP IN THE HOOD LAGOON

Ila Geno

WHAT WE CAN LEARN FROM TRADITIONAL LEADERSHIP?

'Traditional leadership was based on the character of the person as shown by his wealth and how he used it. Wealth came in the forms of land ownership; gardens (through hard work); the number of domestic animals, especially pigs; and the number of valuable trees such as coconut, betel nut and other trees. All of the leader's wealth was public knowledge to the community.

'More important was the leader's ability to share all of this wealth with his family and the village at times of feasting festivals. The leader earned his leadership position by sharing his wealth.

'The community witnessed this. They saw that he collected his wealth from his own properties, unlike wealth deposited in a bank or wealth given to him by some other person. The good thing about traditional leadership was that a leader earned his position by sheer hard work from his own sweat, not through some other person's contributions.

'In other words, traditional leadership worked through a very open system of gaining leadership not conducive to corrupt influences.'

WHAT MAKES A GOOD LEADER IN THE VILLAGE?

'A good leader must be transparent and must work hard to maintain his leadership. He is dependable for the weak people who may have come for help, assisting them with garden food. He must demonstrate that he is independent in terms of survival and does not rely on others for his upkeep with food and other material goods. As well, he is skilful and knowledgeable about the history of the community, in particular on land ownership issues, and he assists the

Pigs all over PNG have been a sign of wealth and a necessary part of leadership. Are pigs still important for leaders in your area today?

community to resolve land disputes and other related issues as well. He must be seen to be fair and to demonstrate integrity.'

WHAT WERE THE GOOD PARTS OF TRADITIONAL LEADERSHIP?

'Traditional leadership was open leadership. The traditional leader's position very much depended on the sharing of his wealth with the people, especially during feasting festivals. There were fewer opportunities for leaders to be corrupt as they dealt with their own hard-earned wealth to assist other people in need. Traditional leaders did not rely on other people to make them leaders; they earned it through their sheer hard work and sweat.'

TRADITIONAL LEADERS HAD TO DEAL WITH CHANGE. THEY HAD TO ADAPT AS COLONIAL POWER MOVED IN. DO YOU KNOW AN EXAMPLE OF PEOPLE WHO DID THAT WELL?

'Early missionaries first arrived to pacify the country and colonial government patrols followed suit. Traditional leaders did well in a number of villages along the Papuan coast. This included the Hood Lagoon villages of Keapara, Alukuni and Karawa in Rigo, Central Province.

'In 1894 or thereabouts, the village leader of the Amoa clan of Hood Lagoon, Mr Airaka Alai, gave a portion of the Amoa Numa family's land to the London Missionary Society to settle on at Hood Lagoon. This was the base for them to conduct missionary work in the area. Without any prior knowledge, Mr Airaka Alai out of wisdom and love accepted and permitted the missionaries to settle on the Amoa Numa family land known as *kele iruna*.

'As the result of that decision, the London Missionary Society established the first permanent foundation for Christianity in Hood Lagoon. They commenced the teaching of a strong Christian influence, which spread very quickly around Hood Lagoon and then came to Hula areas some time later.'

2 TRADITIONAL LEADERSHIP ON MUSSAU ISLAND

Jennifer Litau

THE ROLE OF MATRIARCHAL LEADERSHIP

Leadership on Mussau Island in New Ireland was traditionally based on a matriarchal system. The leadership of women in the community was respected.

One of the women's traditional roles was in agricultural production. As producers, women with rights and control of land boundaries allocated portions of land to male relatives. For example, the land could be used to build a house or plant a garden or chop a tree to build a house or canoe. In doing this, women helped young males to become skilled and independent to marry and care for a family.

Women could decide that elderly men should not hand out portions of land unless they consulted with female landowners. Sometimes when men failed to consult, they gave land to their favourite son and not a daughter. Female leaders worked for fairness between sons and daughters.

THE VALUE OR ETHIC OF BEING CONSIDERATE

Also women were considerate of the community and used their good land to grow extra food crops. This ensured there was plenty of food for:

- each of the community's families
- each of the leaders' families
- making large donations of food to fulfil community needs and festivities.

RESPONSIBILITIES TO THE NEXT GENERATION

Traditional women leaders took care to keep their traditional knowledge safe. They passed knowledge on to the younger generation, especially to responsible female family members. They encouraged the next generation to take good care of the knowledge about family history, their land and inheritance. These female leaders were respected and honoured for their fairness to all in the community.

MOTHERS AS LEADERS IN A MATRIARCHY

Traditional women's leadership covered the natural roles of motherhood. Mothers were known to love, care, respect, share with and help one another. They encouraged the younger generation to do the same. In this they were leaders, as the practice of these values held the community together.

Elderly mothers and women were considered wiser than all if they raised good children to be useful adult men and women. This was good for the community. Children learned women's and men's work from their mothers and fathers. But women had to instil values and insist that children pick these up.

When children turned out well, it was a credit to the leadership and role modelling of their mothers. The words and actions of these women were copied and followed by younger members of the family and clan.

As reproducers, women leaders were respected, obeyed and honoured, and elderly male relatives even consulted and treated them with dignity. They enjoyed high social status.

THE IMPORTANCE OF PROVIDING FOOD FOR FEASTS AND FESTIVITIES

Plentiful food is very important to traditional culture. A good leader fulfilled food obligations. This was witnessed in community festivities such as marriages and deaths.

Large food contributions were expected of family or clan matriarchs. With the help of their family or clan, these women leaders contributed up to 100 cooked taro (suma) baskets, from 10 to 50 bundles of uncooked taro, and just as many bunches of ripe bananas and baskets of cooked fish. Such a contribution showed their skills and strength in organisation, food crop cultivation and preparation, generosity, cooking and high family or clan respect and support. This was highly valued by all, and honourable processions would be made to show off the foodstuff, with the women leading the procession to the festive site. Elders of the community inspected and knew true leaders because they gave their best to the community.

EXPLORE

These two examples provide two views of traditional leadership. Compare the two views:

- What traditional values or ethics have been important to communities?
- Can you find examples of these values in your own community?

Leadership has traditional ethics at all levels. You can find traditional elements everywhere. At the same time, some leaders seem distant from the people, who still survive using much of their traditional knowledge.

STRETCH YOUR THINKING

Do your own study of traditional leadership in your area. You can use the four questions from the first example above (Hood Lagoon):

- What can we learn from traditional leadership?
- What makes a good leader in the village?
- What were the good parts of traditional leadership?
- Traditional leaders had to deal with change. They had to adapt as colonial power moved in. Do you know an example of people who did that well?

You can also use or adapt the subtitles of the second example above (Mussau Island):

- The role of matriarchal leadership
- The value or ethic of being considerate
- Responsibilities to the next generation

- Mothers as leaders in a matriarchy
- The importance of providing food for feasts and festivities

Combine or adapt the materials to make your own study. Analyse your findings. Make two conclusions to answer these two final question sets:

1 What values, practices and knowledge from traditional leadership are still useful? What is valuable to keep?
2 What parts of traditional leadership are not useful now? What should we throw away?

FOR YOURSELF

- If you become a leader, how hard do you think it will be?
- Can you follow the traditional values you think leaders should keep?
- Would you stop using the values you think should be thrown away?

CHAPTER 5

TRADITIONAL APPROACHES TO RESOURCES

Unit 1 for Grade 10 is about resources. It focuses on natural or physical resources. There is extensive traditional and community knowledge about:

- renewable and non-renewable resources
- changes to resources and resource use.

Papua New Guinea is a resource-rich country. People have used New Guinea's resources for 50 000 years. Today you can see changes in resources all around you. You can also find many examples of resources that have been used for thousands of years.

TRADITIONAL NON-RENEWABLE RESOURCES

There are few non-renewable traditional resources. There are minerals that traditional people used, including different ochres. These are rocks with iron in them that can be used to produce different colours. This use was so limited that there was never a risk of running out. Today mining of limonite, one type of ochre, is being considered commercially.

Obsidian was a valuable traditional non-renewable resource traded far into the distant Pacific Islands. Obsidian is a type of glass made by volcanoes. It was used for knives, adzes, axes and other blades.

A greenstone axe is now a valuable artefact for collectors. It is also illegal to export them from Papua New Guinea. But there are still many for sale around the world. Do you think that helps to protect them or hurts this heritage item?

Traditional mining was for obsidian. Again, this non-renewable resource was plentiful. There was never a risk that it would run out. There are boulder beaches of it on Fergusson Island where the ocean is slowly wearing the resource away. There are many other sites for it, but there are many places where it is not found. For that reason, it was a scarce resource to many people. The traditional result was that it was traded far and wide.

Various other tools and items have traditionally been made from stone. Technically this material is non-renewable. Again, traditional use was limited. The artefacts were scarce because they took time, skill and knowledge to make. For example, greenstone axes and adzes were highly valued, but there was never an issue of over-mining or using up the resource with the traditional technologies available.

EXPLORE

- What is the history of non-renewable resources in your area?
- Are any of them still being used?
- Do you or does anyone else in your community have any idea how to make them?
- How important is knowledge about them?

Stone bowls, mortars and pestles have been found in many parts of Papua New Guinea. They have been found in the Highlands, Momase, Oro and the Islands. This tradition stopped probably with the introduction of the sweet potato. No one is sure what the bowls and pestles mean or what they were used for. They may have bird or other animal figures carved on them. This stone pestle was probably used for pounding food at special feasts. It comes from Oro Province.

TRADITIONAL RENEWABLE RESOURCES

Community knowledge about renewable resources existed in all parts of the country. People understood their biosphere and all the resources it held.

Perhaps the first renewable resource that the earliest people saw was trees on the horizon. Traditional people created an agricultural system based on trees. Perhaps early in the use of hunting and gathering, people started to care for trees. This led to what is called *agroforestry* or *arboriculture*. This practice relied on trees for food and many other products.

The first renewable resource that the earliest settlers saw in New Guinea could have been trees. Ever since, people have found many uses for trees and carried them to distant Pacific Islands.

Coconuts, pandanus, tropical almonds, breadnut and breadfruit are just some of the trees used in this system. We will look at a few of these trees. We start with the one that grows from the coast to the mountains: the pandanus. You will see how different places use this renewable resource differently. Then you can search for other uses for this resource from your community or others who know about it.

PANDANUS

Different types of pandanus trees are found across Papua New Guinea. Seeds may have floated on natural rafts from Asia to the Pacific Islands. They may also have been carried to new places by flying foxes or other animals that eat them.

There are about 600 different types of pandanus trees in the world. They have been used in other countries as a resource too. For example, people in India use parts of their pandanus trees for food and mats.

In Papua New Guinea there are two main types of pandanus. You can find coastal pandanus in the lowlands. The fruit is round and the tree grows to about seven metres. In the Highlands, the pandanus is much taller, up to sixteen metres. The Highlands pandanus fruit is oblong. It can be nearly a metre long.

EXPLORE

- What type of pandanus grows in your area?
- What uses can you think of that people have for it?

Now let's explore some examples of how pandanus is used traditionally around Papua New Guinea.

Food

The Highlands pandanus tree is an important source of food. It has very nutritious fruit. The fruit is rich in protein. Meat is another protein source, but meat is often scarce in some villages. This makes the Highlands pandanus tree a valuable food resource. The fruit can be eaten raw or it can be smoked to help preserve it. People crack the nuts open with their teeth or a rock.

The fruit of the coastal pandanus can be eaten too. Often it is cooked. It is not a common food. Aboriginal groups in Australia used the lowland pandanus as a food source. They knew how to prepare it. Colonial Australians did not know how to use it. The famous Australian explorers Burke and Wills died of starvation in outback Australia. They tried to eat pandanus but did not know how to prepare it. They did not ask the Aboriginal people, who saved the last member of their group.

The fruit of the Highlands pandanus is rich in protein. This leads people to claim, care for and protect these trees, both in their gardens and in the forest.

In some places, pandanus leaves are wrapped around food before it is cooked. They add to the flavour. But leaves have many more uses than just cooking.

Roofing

Pandanus is still an important resource for roofs in many villages. The leaves are picked, softened and sown to make sections of roof. These sections are then tied to the roof frame and trusses. A well-maintained roof can last about five years. Then it has to be replaced.

People are changing to metal roofs in some places where they have access to cash. The advantage of a metal roof is that it lasts longer. But metal roofs are hotter in hot weather. The advantage of pandanus roofs is that they are cooler. They provide more insulation in hot weather. They may also cost less if labour and materials are abundant.

Here a man stitches together green pandanus leaves for roof panels. This work is done by men or women in different parts of Papua New Guinea.

EXPLORE

- What traditional roofing materials can you find in your area?
- What imported materials are used for roofing in your area?
- Why do people prefer one or the other?
- Are imported roofs better? Are they a better status symbol?

STRETCH YOUR THINKING

Compare the advantages and disadvantages of using traditional and modern roofing materials. You may try to compare the costs. Think of the time, labour, food and social obligations that may be needed to erect a traditional roof. Compare this with the cost of erecting an imported roof. What conclusions can you make about the use of traditional roofing materials?

Mats and weaving

Pandanus leaves have been used for many years across the Pacific Islands for making mats. Some of the very finest weaving uses thin strips of leaves. The people of Tuvalu were famous for such fine mats. Today, hardly any are made in Tuvalu. This craft may disappear in parts of the Pacific. But it is still strong in Papua New Guinea.

The weaving is generally done by women. You can find different traditional patterns in different parts of our country. People may use imported or local dyes for the colours in the different patterns. Mat-weaving uses a traditional resource as its base. People can also adapt new ideas to mats.

A woman works on making a mat in the Trobriand Islands.

Pandanus leaves are woven for other purposes. They are used to make bags in some places. The Tolai *rat* is a bag like a bilum, used in East New Britain.

EXPLORE

- Are pandanus mats available in your area?
- Who makes them?
- Do people make them for sale or for family use?
- How important are mats in the cultures of your area?
- What type of decorations and patterns are used in local mats?
- Can you find out how these have changed over time?
- Does it matter to tradition and local knowledge if people are using imported or local dyes for colours?
- What other items can you find that are woven from pandanus leaves?

Medicine

Pandanus trees produce some traditional medicines. People still use these in parts of Papua New Guinea. There are various reasons for this. In some places people may not have the income to buy medicines. They may not have access to medicines at an aid post. Or they may find the traditional medicines seem as good as imported ones.

On the north coast of Oro Province people use a pandanus root for medicine. The root is cut. The cut part is capped with a coconut cup. The cup collects liquid dripping from the root. People drink this to ease a sore throat and coughing. The picture shows an uncut root and a cut, capped root.

EXPLORE

- What other traditional medical uses for pandanus can you find?
- How important is pandanus as a medical resource in your area?

Torches

Pandanus roots are made into torches in some places. Use a map to find the settlement of Agaun in the Owen Stanley Ranges. It is in Central Province, just on the border with Milne Bay, high in the mountains. People in the surrounding villages will chop a piece of pandanus root about a metre to a metre-and-a-half long. Then they cut it into thin strips. These are called *tapers*. They dry the tapers and bundle them together. The result is a very bright torch to use at night.

An Agaun man uses a pandanus torch to hunt frogs on a dark night in the mountains. The torch is bright enough to light up the frogs' eyes. Frogs are another traditional food resource.

EXPLORE

Pandanus trees have many uses. The text has shown you some. What other uses can you discover for pandanus trees?

- Can you find any use for this resource that is growing?
- Can you find any uses that are disappearing or have already stopped?
- How many ways do *you* use pandanus?

We will return to the pandanus in Chapter 6 when we look at conservation and protection of resources.

Coastal pandanus are common in many parts of Papua New Guinea and have various uses.

STRETCH YOUR THINKING

- How is this resource used differently by men and women in your area?
- What roles do men play in the use of this resource?
- What roles do women play in the use of this resource?
- When do men and women combine to use the resource?
- Is the resource more important for women or for men? Or is it equally important to both?

SAGO

The sago palm is an important traditional source of food for some groups in Papua New Guinea. People may also go back to collecting sago when money is short for buying food or when other foods become less available. Sago has various other uses as well. Again, you can look at how traditional use is changing and consider what is happening to sago as a traditional food.

Sago is limited to growing in lowland areas and needs plenty of water. It is often found in or near swamps. People may produce and sell sago for cash.

Extracting the starch

Traditional knowledge has long been used to extract starch from the trunk of the sago palm. The tree is cut down and the trunk is split open. The pith is chopped out and washed with fresh water. Today almost everyone uses metal to smash out the pith. Long ago people would have used stone or wooden tools to extract the starch kernels.

The pictures on the next page show people extracting sago in Oro Province. Different places have different systems. For example, in Manus sago is made by men and women taking different roles in the process. Men chop down the tree. Then tasks are divided. Men will beat the sago while the women do the washing and drain the water. This collects the final residue, which looks like a white flour. Women place it into long baskets for smoking and drying to make it ready for consumption.

The sago pith is removed from the tree.

The pith is washed in a sluice to extract the starch.

The traditional way to carry water to the sluice to extract the starch.

The starch is concentrated and will now be wrapped in banana leaves and cooked.

Ways to cook sago

The most important traditional use for sago is as a food. It is still a staple in some areas where people remain self-sufficient. This starch is used in many different ways of cooking. Here are some examples:

- During feasts in Manus, women prepare the sago. In other places, this role may be taken by men. For feasts in Manus, sago can be fried mixed with coconut oil, or fried in a mixture of heavy coconut milk, or just fried dry. It can also be made into sago dumplings, cakes or puddings.
- In parts of Western Province, large sago puddings are cooked up for special feasts and celebrations.
- In Oro Province and the Sepik, sago is baked or fried into pancake-shaped foods. These are often eaten with fish.

EXPLORE

- What other ways can you find in which sago is used as a food?
- What other traditional ways can you find for cooking it?
- Can you find examples of imported sago? If there is a food store in your area, you can look for packets of dried pudding mixes, or other mixes that may have sago as a thickener.

Other uses for sago palms

Sago palm fronds are used for thatching roofs on some traditional homes. Like pandanus, sago fronds can last for about five years if maintained. In some traditional cultures, people called a house 'hot' if it was lived in and maintained. They called a house 'cold' if it was not lived in and maintained. A cold house could fall down in just a couple of years.

The sago beetle grub feeds on sago pith. People will eat this grub. Sometimes they will help it grow in the sago. It is very nutritious with plenty of protein.

DISCUSS

- Do people prefer sago or pandanus or another roofing material in your area?
- What traditional ways do you know that people used to maintain a traditional house?
- Do they use the terms 'hot' and 'cold' to describe houses in your area?
- Why do you think people would call a house hot?
- What tradition do you think that refers to?

There are other uses for the sago palm. For example, the stalks of the palm fronds can be dried and used for making walls. Can you discover any other uses for the sago palm?

Here sago made traditionally is on sale. Does this make it a cash crop? What does this photograph tell you about how people are adapting traditional knowledge to new uses?

BREADNUT TREE

The breadnut tree looks similar to a breadfruit tree, but the fruit is filled with seeds (or nuts). The seeds can be eaten and are a good protein source. Or the fruit can be eaten while it is still immature. Then the nut or seed portion is still soft. The fruit is often cut up and cooked in a soup.

The breadnut tree is the ancestor of the breadfruit tree. The Lapita people may have bred breadfruit trees from breadnut trees during their time in New Guinea. Breadfruit trees were then spread across the Pacific Islands by the early settlers.

There are other uses for the breadnut tree. They are similar to the breadfruit, so we will go straight to it.

BREADFRUIT TREE

Breadfruit, like some types of yam, banana and sugarcane, is indigenous to New Guinea. It spread across the Pacific as an important food source for the original settlers of the Pacific Islands. The tree provides nutritious food. The fruit is mainly a carbohydrate with vitamins and minerals. The fruit can be boiled, baked or roasted. You could explore traditional ways to cook the fruit and seeds.

The tree has many other traditional uses. Here are some. Maybe you can find more if breadfruit is grown in your area:

- **Timber.** The breadfruit produces a light timber that can be used for construction, as a fuel wood from old or dying trees, and for small canoes.
- **Glue.** The sap is white and sticky. It can be used as glue.
- **Traditional medicine.** Smashed up leaves and/or sap may be used to treat skin problems, and small quantities of sap mixed with water may be used to stop diarrhoea symptoms (although this may not cure the illness) and ease stomach aches. The bark, sap and leaves have other traditional medicinal uses.
- **Rope** can be made from the inner bark.

The scientific name for the bread**nut** tree is *Artocarpus camansi*. The name for the bread**fruit** tree is *Artocarpus altilis*. Scientific names are written in Latin. Both trees are called *kapiak* in Tok Pisin. Are there special names for them in your area? Do people have different names for them and their different varieties?

COCONUT

Along the coast, the most important tree traditionally for New Guinea and the Pacific Islands is the coconut. The coconut is a tree with many uses. Here is a list of some ways it was used traditionally:

- food for humans and animals
- fibre for ropes to lash outrigger canoes
- palm fronds woven for baskets, temporary sleeping mats and food holders
- palm fronds for roofs and shade walls
- timber for homes and other buildings
- inner coconut cup for holding liquids (including body paints or tattoo ink)
- oil in a few traditional cases.

*The coconut palm has many traditional uses. It is a vital resource for many villagers. It is used in traditional medicine in some places. Chewing on a coconut root can help to stop diarrhoea (*pekpek wara*). But this is only curing a symptom. If it is a serious infection, this traditional treatment may not be enough.*

Niu is the word for coconut in many Austronesian languages. The small Pacific Island state of Niue is named after the coconut. Roughly translated, *niue* means 'Wow! Coconuts!'

This resource is now available across much of Papua New Guinea, including the Highlands, through the road system. It has a cash value, although that has gone down over the years.

Coconut plantations used to be very important. There are still some coconut smallholders but copra is losing to oil palm. The coconut is slipping back to being more a traditional item than a cash crop. There are still markets for copra, but they have been declining for many years.

Village copra production has fallen along with copra prices.

The village copra smoker is used less these days, but it still works for villages that have few or no other ways to earn cash.

You may wish to explore the many traditions connected to village use of coconuts. You can find some of these traditions in the cities as well. All parts of the coconut have some traditional use.

EXPLORE

- See how many different uses you can find and make a list. Then write a paragraph on which ones remain important.
- Give your ideas on what the future of the coconut may be. Consider what newer uses there are for the coconut. (For example, can you find things made from coconut timber?)

TAHITIAN CHESTNUT OR PAPUAN BISCUIT

A common name for this tree in the Pacific is Tahitian chestnut. In parts of PNG it is also called the Papuan biscuit. The scientific name for it is *Inocarpus fagifer* (remember, scientific names are written in Latin). It probably came originally from South-East Asia and has been used in New Guinea for thousands of years. It is part of the collection of trees, plants and animals that traditional colonists carried from New Guinea starting some 3000 years ago across the Pacific.

There are various names for this food tree. Some people call it a Papuan biscuit tree. Others call it the Tahitian chestnut. It is called aila *in Tok Pisin.*

The main purpose of this tree is for food. Food comes from the seed pod. The pod contains both carbohydrate and protein. There are many ways to cook it.

The tree has other uses. The timber is easy to carve and can also be used for light construction. The leaves and bark have been used in traditional medications. Where fuel is scarce, it can be used as a fuel wood (especially any dead branches).

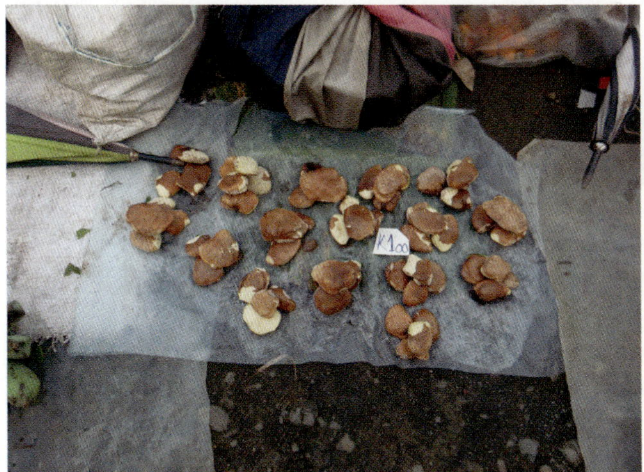

The edible part of the Papuan biscuit can be boiled in water or coconut milk. It can be smashed up to make a pudding with other traditional ingredients. Baking or grilling are two other traditional ways to cook this food.

OTHER TREE PRODUCTS

Another way to explore the use of traditional trees is to start with tree products. Here we look at some of the products traditionally made from trees. These will vary from place to place. As a study in resources and traditional resource use, you can trace any wooden or other tree product back to its source. Here are the steps for a simple study:

- Identify the traditional item.
- Identify the traditional tree it comes from (the original physical resource).
- Describe the traditional technologies used to make it.
- What is happening to the tree now?
- Is it threatened by forest clearing or something else?
- Is the traditional product still being made? Is it losing or gaining value?
- Is the use of the traditional product changing?

Tapa cloth

Let's take tapa cloth as an example. The traditional technology for making tapa starts with the bark being taken from a young tree or trees. It is stripped off the tree. Then it is cleaned up and soaked in water to soften it.

Tapa is made from the inner bark of the paper mulberry tree. The scientific name for this tree is Broussonetia papyrifera. *Tapa can also be made from other trees. For example, it is made from some types of breadfruit trees. Other tree barks are traditionally used for clothing and rain shields in Papua New Guinea.*

Next, a process of beating the bark starts. The bark must be flattened and spread out. Then it can be folded over itself and pounded more. The process continues. In Papua New Guinea, the custom is to make one long sheet.

The finished tapa cloth may be used 'as is'. Often it is decorated with traditional paints and dyes. These can be made from many natural resources. They include berries, ochre, natural inks, roots and other local products. Each group or clan will have its own special patterns or images for decorating tapa.

For the traditional technology, men and women may have different roles in making tapa. For example, stripping the tapa bark free can be men's work in many places. Pounding and making the tapa tends to be women's work.

The paper mulberry tree comes from southern China. Austronesian people carried the seeds of this tree to Papua New Guinea. It probably took them two or three thousand years to travel south to New Guinea. Austronesians then carried these seeds to places like Tonga, Vanuatu and Fiji where you can find tapa still made today. However, it is probably still most used by Papua New Guineans as an important traditional resource.

EXPLORE

- Can you find examples of tapa in your area?
- Can you trace the process back to the tree?
- Can you find decorated tapa cloth?
- Can you find what the decorations represent or mean to the traditional makers?
- Can you find who is responsible for making the decorations?
- If tapa is not used in your area, can you find other traditional examples of bark clothing? (See also page 91 to continue the theme of traditional clothing.)

Other traditional tree products

Below are a few other traditional tree products. You will be able to find many more. Can you trace the process of their construction back to the tree or trees involved?

MOVING CANOES

You can also explore the traditional technologies for hauling large canoes up onto beaches. It is similar to transporting large canoes from where they were made to the water. The most ingenious is the canoe ladder. This system uses small logs or large straight branches to roll the canoe on. A very large canoe can be taken from the forest to the water using this system.

Canoe trees *come in various sizes and types depending on the canoe and place where it is made. This resource has provided transport to the far Pacific in the past. Canoe trees are still an important resource in many places. Are canoe trees scarce or abundant where you live? And what about the paddle and other parts of the canoe? What special trees are used for these items?*

The ***garamut*** *or slit gong is a traditional instrument still used for communication and festivals in different places. Here is a garamut from East Sepik. Only certain trees can be used to make a garamut. Do you know what they are in your area? Is the garamut a tradition that is disappearing in your area? Does that matter?*

Here is a garamut that is used to call people to church on Tami Island. What do you think the carving might be? How is the tradition staying the same and how is it changing? Does this help tell some of the Tami Islanders who they are?

String and rope *can be made from the bark of various trees (including the coconut) and other plants. In this picture you see the tree limb that the bark has been taken from.*

Next you strip out the fibre to use in rope making. This rope is to be used for lashing together parts of an outrigger canoe. Can you find tree bark used for fibre in your area? What other uses can you find for tree bark?

Homes and other traditional buildings

Many people live in traditional homes. There are various styles using different plant products.

Coastal homes often have an outbuilding for daily use and a sleeping haus *that gives more protection at night. The outbuildings are open to stay cool. This is an example from East Sepik. A friend from another village has come to visit. A similar structure is the* oro *or* haus win *found in Oro Province.* Oro *means welcome. It is a place to welcome friends and stay cool or dry, depending on the weather.*

On the coast and in lowland areas where flooding can occur, houses are generally built on stilts. This also helps keep them cool in a hot tropical climate. Some homes and outbuildings have no walls. This too helps keep them cool. Other homes do have walls. These can be made of sago, nipa palm leaves, pandanus leaves, bamboo, bark or planks. The roof is insulated against the tropical sun. You have seen roofing materials from various trees on previous pages.

Here is a Highlands house where timber planks are not fitted closely together. An inner wall of woven bamboo is visible. Iron sheeting protects the bottom. Wall material and timber are in the foreground. The roof is a thick layer of grass for extra insulation. What reasons can you think of for this construction?

Here a Highland home is locked for security. Security of people and homes has always been a concern across Papua New Guinea. What traditional approaches to security can you find? How are these changing?

In the Highlands, many traditional homes are round. Planks are driven into the ground. They are fitted tightly together. This is for protection from other people and from the cold. Some traditional technologies also use insulation to hold heat in the traditional Highland home. Traditional insulation could be made of grass, bark and other plant materials.

MEN'S AND WOMEN'S HOUSES

Traditionally in the Highlands, men and women were separated. All parts of New Guinea traditionally had a men's *haus*. Older boys and younger men were kept separate. Some houses could be very large, such as the *haus tambaram* of the Sepik.

Today you can find traditional house construction mixed with imported materials. The first picture shows an example from the coast. The second picture shows the inside of a Highlands home. What do these two photos tell you about traditions adapting new materials? What does this tell you about who you are?

GETTING TREE RESOURCES WHERE TREES ARE SCARCE

The mainland of Papua New Guinea was resource rich for traditional people. On isolated atolls there are fewer natural resources. One way they improved the resource base was salvaging trees that had been washed from the mainland out to sea. The trees could be used for timber and some provided stone trapped in the root system for stone tools.

Rocks trapped in the root system of a tree. Both the tree and the rocks are valuable natural resources on atolls.

Small islands may have some trees, but the people collect further tree resources from the sea. Here salvaged timbers are being dried for various uses.

Tami Island is famous for its carving. There are very few trees on Tami Island. The material for carving comes from trees washed out from the PNG mainland. Here are examples of two beautifully carved Tami Island bowls.

Today people call this tree the steel wool tree. They use the leaves to clean pots and pans. In the past they used it to clean and/or smooth wooden items. What plants or trees do you know of or can find for cleaning and smoothing items like wood?

Many other uses for trees

You should be able to find many other trees and tree products in your area. How are uses changing? How many different traditional ways to use the plants of your area can you find?

Changes to the traditional treescape

Trees are a vital resource to the people of Papua New Guinea. Many are now both a traditional and a modern resource. A lot of trees have been exported for timber. This means the traditional resource is lost. In some places the exported trees have been replaced with a new tree resource. Two of the newest imported tree resources are oil palm and balsa.

Oil palm trees are an import to Papua New Guinea. They replace traditional tree resources and provide cash for some. They also remove the traditional trees that were a vital resource for village survival. Here you see mature oil palms in the background and newly planted oil palms in the foreground. This is in a mixed plantation and block holder system. Some villagers will earn cash from it.

Balsa is another tree imported to Papua New Guinea as a cash crop. It is a fast-growing tree. It comes originally from the Amazon region in South America. Again, monoculture replaces arboriculture or agroforestry.

EXPLORE

- What other trees can you find that have been imported to Papua New Guinea?
- What has been the effect of imported trees in your area?
- Has the introduction of these new trees changed the resource use of traditional tree resources in your area?

EXPLORING NEWER TRADITIONS

The idea of a plantation is an imported idea to Papua New Guinea. Some of the trees for plantations are imported. These include coffee, cacao, rubber and oil palm.

Coffee provides a good example of people starting new traditions. They are creating local knowledge. At the same time, coffee sales are linked to an international market. Highlanders began taking coffee beans or seedlings from plantations about 60 years ago. That was in the 1950s. They developed a smallholder system of coffee production. People in other areas also started smallholder production and this continues in parts of the Owen Stanley Mountains.

The Highlander coffee tree is tough. It can go for years with little or no care if the market for coffee is poor. Highlanders treat the trees better when markets are good. They have developed a system or tradition for producing coffee that is their own.

Who might be growing this coffee? What hints does the picture give to help you guess what type of agriculture this is? What principles of Melanesian arboriculture do you see?

Highlander smallholder coffee farming is very different from the plantation system. The smallholders use different planting materials. They use different planting systems. They use different pruning systems. They plant on traditionally owned land. They use various labour systems. But the system is linked to global agricultural markets. It is the base of one of many newer PNG traditions.

STRETCH YOUR THINKING

Choose any plantation crop that is also grown by smallholders. Compare the plantation and smallholder systems. Can you find new PNG traditions or is it all imported ideas? You may also find block-holders. Analyse how different they are from smallholders.

Compare:

- **Land:** Who owns it? How is treated? What are the landholding traditions?
- **Labour:** Where does the labour come from? How is labour paid? What traditions can you find in the way labour works?
- **Investment:** Who makes an investment in the resource? What types of investment are made? Explore the differences between investing money in the resource and other investments to make the resource grow.
- **The tree crop:** How is the crop treated? Where does the crop come from? How do people access planting material? What strategies or systems do people use to maintain the crop? Is it strictly a monoculture?
- **Your conclusion:** Are traditions increasing or dying for smallholder cash crops? What do you think the future will be for smallholder cash crops?

Other plants that are being used in both traditional and new ways

Coffee is just one newer resource where community or traditional knowledge has been part of its success for smallholders. Newer food crops such as peanuts, cassava and corn have found their way into traditional gardens. There are also traditional plant products that are being used to raise cash. Consider the following two examples and then seek out your own.

Corn or maize is an interesting crop. It comes from the Americas. It was taken to Europe by Spaniards some 400 years ago. The Native Americans knew how to use corn. They had built a tradition of treating it with lime (the kind eaten with buai*). This kept vitamin B in the corn. Europeans did not use that tradition. This caused serious health problems in places where they ate only corn as the staple. They suffered from a disease known as pellagra. It could kill. Papua New Guineans get vitamin B from leafy greens and other foods.*

You will be able to find examples all around you of traditional tree resources being used in new ways. The introduction of a cash economy is one place to look. Consider this picture. The women are using betel nuts and coconut products to earn cash. What traditional skills are they applying here? How are they saving money doing this? How are they making money? What does this tell you about how Papua New Guineans are using community knowledge?

Trees are just one area of renewable resources used in Papua New Guinea. We have covered some of the major ones. We did not look at bananas although they would have been part of the early tree agriculture systems. Bananas are a giant herb or grass. You can study them.

OTHER TRADITIONAL RESOURCES AND SYSTEMS

There are many other plants, animals and resources from the sea and the earth. Some we will mention in the next chapter on conservation. Others you will have to explore on your own. Examples of using these resources are animal husbandry and exploiting sea resources. These are areas for your research.

AGRICULTURAL SYSTEMS

The first agricultural systems were probably based on trees. There are other traditional agricultural systems dating to some 9000 years ago in the Highlands. You can explore any of these:

- **Shifting cultivation.** Slash-and-burn, swidden or shifting cultivation is still practised in many parts of the country. Taro, yams, sugarcane, bananas, greens, cassava, sweet potato and other crops are traditionally grown using this system. As agriculture intensifies, these crops can then be grown in larger quantities in the two systems described below.
- **Drainage and irrigation systems.** Drainage and irrigation systems are another traditional approach to agriculture. Remember that Kuk, the ancient site in the Highlands, shows evidence of a complicated drainage system. All evidence points to taro as the main crop grown there. However, looking at traditional Highlands agriculture, you would suspect there was much more grown than just taro.

- **Agricultural intensification.** Population pressure (see Chapter 2) leads to more intensive agriculture. This is demonstrated in the Highlands. Populations grew too large for slash-and-burn agriculture. More intensive systems resulted. Sweet potato mounding is one response. Terrace systems for agriculture have also been found in the Highlands. They were again probably used for taro.
- **House gardens.** House gardens are another type of traditional agriculture. These are still common although many traditional plants are no longer grown. In the Highlands, a house garden in the past had could have up to 60 different plants. There were plants for medicines, foods, clothing, decoration and other uses.

House gardens are still found all over Papua New Guinea in both rural and urban settings. They often have a mix of traditional and imported plants. What plants do you see in this garden?

THINKING FURTHER ABOUT TRADITIONAL RESOURCES

TRADITIONAL MEDICINE: YOUR ANALYSIS

Today many Papua New Guineans find it hard to pay for medicines and hospital treatment. Some are going back to traditional medicine and traditional healers. Sometimes the traditional cures work. Sometimes traditional remedies only cure the symptoms, not the disease.

Sometimes traditional cures do not work. For example, traditional medicine cannot cure HIV/AIDS, tuberculosis, yaws, poor eyesight, malaria or cholera. Only imported drugs and treatments can cure these types of disease.

Sometimes people mix imported treatments with traditional treatments. They may go to the hospital for imported drugs. Outside they may find a traditional healer who gives them traditional treatment. The healer may seem to pull a little bat or insect from the sick person's body. The healer tells them this was causing the pain. If a person believes this, they may feel better.

EXPLORE

Choose some common health problems in your area (for example, grille, pneumonia, dengue fever, tropical ulcers, flu or colds). Or choose another area of health such as treatments for broken bones, childbirth or mental health. Compare traditional and imported approaches.

1 Make a list of treatments in your area.
2 Look at both imported and traditional treatment. Compare the costs. Compare how easy it is to get the treatment (how available is it?).
3 Consider:
   - What treatments seem to work?
   - What treatments do not seem to work?
   - Are there differences in treatments for men and women, boys and girls?
   - Are some people mixing traditional and modern treatments?
   - Are some people getting no treatment at all?
4 Write a paragraph of your conclusions. Are there areas where traditional treatments seem to work? Are there links between traditional and imported treatments? Do some people have no choice of treatment? Are males and females treated differently? What is needed in your area to improve human health?

This picture shows a common coastal shrub. Here is one of its uses: people use its leaves to wash their face and clean their eyes before spearfishing in the sea. It is a simple traditional aid. Consider:

- Is it a medicine? What would you call it?
- Can you find other uses if you are on the coast, or similar cleaning plants away from the coast?
- What about plants with other uses? Which ones are medical? Which ones are aids to doing things?
- Draw them and tell how they are used. Label them with the different names people have for them.

TRADITIONAL CONSERVATION

Unit 2 Grade 10 is about the environment. This is a major area for traditional and community knowledge about:

- the local environment and ways to use it
- protection of the environment
- conservation and preservation of the environment.

THE LOCAL ENVIRONMENT AND WAYS TO USE IT

Traditional knowledge provided everything a person needed to know in order to survive in their environment. You can search out any number of ways people have used their local environment.

One approach is to think of something you or a family member does every day. Then see if you can explain or discover how it was done traditionally. If you want a real challenge, see if you can actually do it.

PREPARING A MEAL THE TRADITIONAL WAY

Let's take an example. Imagine preparing a meal like this:

1. You walk into the kitchen or *haus kuk*.
2. You take a sweet potato or a piece of breadfruit.
3. You place it in a pot.
4. You pour in some water.
5. You light the stove with a match (or turn on the electricity).
6. You put the pot on the heat to cook.
7. You put the cooked food on a plate.
8. You sprinkle a little salt on it.
9. You get yourself a glass of cool water from the refrigerator.
10. You take out some fresh salad greens to eat with the hot food.
11. Finally you sit down to enjoy your simple meal.

Let's break down each step to see how it might be done using the local environment only. (You can explore this example and many more for your own location. You could make a table showing the way it is done now and the traditional way. At each step you can show how people with traditional knowledge know how to use the local environment.)

1 **You walk into the kitchen or *haus kuk*.** The traditional cooking place will be made of local products. Stones and clay may make the hearth. Wood is the fuel. Often in the dry season cooking is just done outside in a mumu pit, over a fire or using hot embers from a fire. In this case we would use the last technique because we are cooking something in water.

EXPLORE

- What are the traditional cooking places and techniques in your area?
- Do some people still use them?
- Are they popular or are they changing?

All over Papua New Guinea people still use the mumu, often now only for special occasions. Mumu cooking can be done for a large or small group. The basis for most mumus is very hot rocks. In very swampy areas of Western Province, a type of mumu is done above ground.

2 **You take a sweet potato to cook.** There are various foods you might take to cook. It could be taro, a banana or a piece of breadfruit. People used the local environment for food production.

EXPLORE

- What traditional agricultural systems are still used in your area? (See Chapter 5 for more information.)
- What foods are produced in your local area?

3 **You place it in a pot.** Traditionally people used clay pots. These are much harder to find now. They are still used in a few villages. Sometimes they are used for special feasts. When people did not have clay in their local environment, they had to trade a resource they had (like smoked wallabies in south Papua) for clay pots. If they could not trade and had no clay, they had to use some other way to cook food.

Clay pots for cooking are rare in much of Papua New Guinea.

EXPLORE

- Can you find a clay pot for cooking? Or can you find a similar container?

NEW POTTERY STYLES

Traditional pottery has now changed in many parts of the country. The pottery is produced for cash. You will still find some potters using traditional clay sources and preparation techniques. Styles and products are now made for new markets. There are examples around Madang, Port Moresby and Kainantu. Can you locate other examples?

The potters of Bilbil village near Madang Town still use traditional technologies to treat and shape the clay. But the final products have new styles and functions. Tradition is being adapted to market forces for cash.

4 **You pour in some water.** Can you get clean water in a traditional way from your environment? Clean water is a valuable resource and many places in the world have very little of it left. Once you locate clean water in your environment you must carry it to the cooking place. A coconut cup is too small and would take too long. Gourds and large bamboo tubes are two types of traditional water carrier.

EXPLORE

- What traditional water carriers did people use in your area?
- How easy is it to traditionally get water from your environment now?
- What imported ideas and products make this task easier?

5 **You light the stove with a match.** You can find many traditional stories about making fire and the first time people learned to cook food. There are many different traditional ways to make a fire. Look at the pictures below to learn about one way.

Here is one way to make fire using friction and dry materials. But you must know your environment well to know what wood to use.

In less than a minute of hard rubbing the friction is enough to start an ember.

Tinder from a coconut and extra oxygen from blowing are used to create a flame from the ember. And it only takes a minute.

EXPLORE

Find out how fire was traditionally made in your area. Record the ways you find and see if you can actually make a fire using only a traditional method. But be careful: only make a small fire and be sure to put it out.

6 **You put the pot on the heat to cook.** You need hot rocks to heat the water. Traditional clay pots were not strong enough to go directly onto fires. People heated rocks in a similar way to heating rocks for a mumu (but sometimes not as long). Gently place the rock in

the pot. If it is hot enough, the water will heat and cook your food. You may also put some hot embers around the base of the pot. But do not put the fire around the pot. That will destroy it and spoil your dinner.

7 **You put the cooked food on a plate.** Traditional food wraps included ferns, banana leaves and breadfruit leaves. All of these could serve as 'plates'. People also ate food off the thin outer part of coconut tree trunks. This is yet another use for coconut fibre. Wooden bowls were used for feasting. Often, however, just your hand was your plate.

8 **You sprinkle a little salt on it.** One way of making salt was to cut down banana suckers or stems. People would soak the banana stems in salty water. The banana stem was then dried and burned. They used the ashes from this process as a form of salt to flavour food.

In some parts of the Highlands there were salt soaks. These were pools of salty water that people used to extract salt. Another way of getting salt in the Highlands was to burn the stems and roots of certain ferns. The fern roots could concentrate scarce salts from the soil. Like burning salt-soaked banana stems on the coast, this could produce a salty ash.

EXPLORE

- Can you make your own salt?
- Look for someone who still remembers how salt was traditionally made in your area and get them to explain the process.

9 **You get yourself a glass of cool water from the refrigerator.** People used various containers for holding water and keeping it cool. Clay pots, bamboo containers and gourds were all common water holders. They all insulate water and can help to keep it cool. A coconut cup was one way to drink water kept cool in a traditional water vessel.

EXPLORE

- What was the traditional way to keep drinking water in your area?
- What items did people use to drink water?

10 **You take out some fresh salad greens to eat with the hot food.** People both grow and collect leafy green vegetables across PNG. These are an important part of the diet as they contain valuable vitamins and minerals. Villagers collect edible water plants from swamps, rivers and streams.

Collecting greens in the wild is still common in some parts of PNG. Growing leafy greens has always been important. Food gardens used to have many different types of leafy greens. Now there are fewer. Some greens need cooking and others are eaten raw.

Near Daulo Pass in the Highlands, a man eats fresh raw greens found on a forest path. People often ate greens where they found them when foraging. This still happens where the resource is plentiful.

EXPLORE

One of the most common leafy green vegetables is aibika. It is easy to grow and delicious to eat. Starting with aibika, make a table of traditional vegetables in your area.

- Which ones are still grown?
- Which ones are collected in the wild?
- What traditions are associated with the different vegetables?
- Who is in charge of growing them?
- Which ones can be eaten raw?
- Which ones must be cooked?
- Who cooks them?
- How do people like them compared with imported vegetables such as carrots, onions, broccoli and cauliflower?

11 **Finally you sit down to enjoy your simple meal.** Eating is still done on traditionally woven mats in many places. Is that a tradition you know? Another tradition was about who ate first and who ate together. Women and small children might eat separately from men. Young men and boys might also cook and eat separately. At feasts, different persons or different groups might eat in different orders or sometimes everyone might eat together.

EXPLORE

- What were the traditional eating practices in your area?
- What differences were there in everyday eating and feasting?
- How was food prepared for different special occasions?
- Who prepared food for everyday use and who prepared it on special occasions?
- How many of these traditions are still practised today?

This is a Highlands plant that was only eaten in soups after a funeral. Its purpose was to give people strength after the difficult time of funerary rites.

OTHER USES OF THE LOCAL ENVIRONMENT

You can try the exercise above with other activities. You can follow a thread using the same method we have just used for preparing food. For instance, how did people get food from the garden to the village?

There are many other ways to look at your local environment and traditional ways to use it. Ask yourself:

- How much are you still using the local environment?
- How much has changed?

Here are two more short examples to help your thinking.

Clothing

Tapa cloth was one traditional material used for dressing. Both men and women used it. Have you heard of a talo*? Can you find examples of them? What about other types of traditional clothing?*

The purpur *is called a 'grass skirt' in English. But it is not made of grass. It is made from many other things, depending on the place. These may include some forms of tree bark, sago leaves, pandanus leaves, special reeds or other vegetable material. Here two young Fergusson Island children wear one type of* purpur.

EXPLORE

- What are traditional skirts made of in your area?
- Can you detail the process? Girls, could you make one?

The bilum and other objects for carrying things

If you go back to Step 2 in the original example, you might ask: How did the sweet potato get to the kitchen? The traditional answer is that someone carried it, and they probably used a bilum.

People made various carrying devices using community knowledge. The most common is the bilum. They come in different sizes for different jobs. They have different patterns in different parts of the country.

Look at the photographs below and then explore bilums and other carrying items in your local area. How are people adapting to making bilums? How are they recycling in making carry bags (which helps conservation)?

Here a woman strings together a bilum. Traditionally women make the string for bilums. The simplest way is rolling it on their thigh with their hand. They might use traditional dyes and designs. There are various types of bilums from large to small, for both men and women. Making a bilum is a skill that women learn. The traditional weave pulls in several directions. This cannot be matched by a machine.

Bilums are made all over the country. Styles and materials are changing. Here a woman recycles material to make a bilum-like bag. How does this help the environment?

Here Highlands women have adapted bilum-making with imported materials and new ideas for uses. The basis is traditional. They sell various traditional bilums. You can see small and large ones. They also sell women's and children's clothing made in a bilum style, and little hats too. This is a cultural innovation. It is using a tradition very cleverly. It is adapting tradition to a cash society.

There are other traditional carry bags that are still commonly used in New Britain and New Ireland. Here is one alongside a new-style bilum.

Here is another type of carry bag made using recycling. It may provide an alternative carry bag to some types of traditional bilum. These were for sale in the Madang Town market.

EXPLORE

- What are the traditional carry bags of your area?
- What materials are used to make them?
- Can you trace back and find the plant for making traditional bilum string? Can you make the string yourself?
- How have materials changed?
- What are the advantages and disadvantages of traditional materials compared with imported materials?
- Detail the way a traditional bilum is put together once the string is ready. Can you make one?
- Which type of bilums do you think may be replaced by other types of bags?
- Which types may not be replaced?
- How valuable are traditional bilums considered in your area?

PROTECTING, CONSERVING AND PRESERVING THE ENVIRONMENT

This part of the chapter explores traditional ways to protect, conserve and preserve the natural environment. We start by looking at how some traditional gardening practices maintain a balance with the environment.

Growing populations put increased pressure on the environment. Traditionally, this meant there was more pressure on foraging for food (that is, hunting, fishing and collecting in the bush). Growing populations came to rely more and more on agricultural systems. Chapter 5 looked at some of the most important trees in traditional arboriculture. Now we look at how shifting agriculture worked to conserve the environment.

SHIFTING AGRICULTURE: SLASH-AND-BURN GARDENING

Slash-and-burn gardening systems rely on cutting, drying and then burning the vegetation. This improves the soil by adding nutrients to it. It makes the first crop very good. But after

Here you see a typical Highlands slash-and-burn (or 'swidden') garden. In fact, not all the trees have been slashed or burnt. You can see that trees have been left and saplings encouraged to grow to conserve the soil and preserve valuable food trees. In this case you can also see the soil mounded for taro. By using mounds, the gardeners are helping to improve the soil using a technique commonly used for sweet potato. This is traditional conservation of soil.

that crops decline. The garden land can only be used for three years at the most. Then new land is needed.

The time the land is not being used is called the *fallow* time. The longer the fallow period is, the more the soil will improve. Further, if trees are allowed to grow up, they will kill grasses and other light-loving weeds. This makes the cleared garden easier to maintain for crops.

The best land is covered by bush and trees. If grass is allowed to take over a fallow garden, the soil will not be as fertile. Traditionally people understood this. They might allow some woody plants to start regrowing as the garden was being used. The objective was to garden and then return the land to woody regrowth. They also might spare some trees from the start.

When garden ground is left fallow, the forest begins to grow again. The process of shifting gardens from one place to another while the forest regrows is a form of conservation. So long as the fallow period is long enough, the natural environment is maintained.

CONSERVING TREES IN TRADITIONAL GARDENS

Slash-and-burn gardening did not actually kill everything. Often people saved trees they thought had value. A tree that produced food, for example, might not be cut down. Or a tree might have some other use as timber or medicine.

People traditionally knew what trees were especially good for improving the soil and would leave them standing. They would often cut off many of the branches so there was plenty of sunlight for the crops. When the garden was finished, the trees would continue to produce. These trees had been conserved or preserved.

Protection and ownership of traditional trees

Traditionally people protected their trees. Managing traditional trees as a food resource is still important in many PNG villages (for example, the pandanus in Highland villages and the breadfruit in coastal villages). Everywhere people have different rights to the use of traditional trees for food and other products. People protect valuable trees. And everywhere, people claim ownership or use rights to trees.

EXPLORE

Explore tree protection using the pandanus or some other important food tree in your area.

- What is the situation of pandanus resources (or other tree resources) in your area?
- How important are ownership and conservation?
- With so many uses, how important is it in your community to care for pandanus trees (or other useful trees)?
- Are they becoming more important or less important?
- What do you think the future for this resource is in Papua New Guinea?
- Are traditional tree products becoming more commercial in your area? (That means are more of them now sold for money?)
- Does a money value help maintain a traditional resource?

SLASH-AND-MULCH SYSTEMS: A TRADITIONAL WAY TO CONSERVE SOIL AND SAVE WORK TIME

The Great Papuan Plateau is an area of rich rainforest and heavy rainfall. It includes Mount Bosavi and is located in Southern Highlands and Western Provinces. It is an area that has attracted conservation concern, especially regarding gas, oil and pipelines.

The Great Papuan Plateau is one of a few places where different peoples have used a traditional system called *slash-and-mulch*. For example, the Etoro and Kaluli peoples are two groups living on the plateau who traditionally used various slash-and-mulch techniques. Slash-and-mulch has also been used in other parts of the forested Highlands and in Manus, and in other parts of Melanesia. The Nduimba people of the Eastern Highlands traditionally used this system in some places.

Slash-and-mulch is a fairly simple system with many benefits where population pressure is low. It is used for growing taro, bananas, sugar cane and other crops. It does not use burning. Rather it uses organic mulch.

WHAT IS MULCH?

Mulch is any protective material put around plants to help them grow. It can be leaves, bark, straw or even stones. Leaves, bark and straw are all examples of organic mulches. Stones are an example of inorganic mulch. Mulches help conserve or protect the soil.

Here is how it works. Some clearing may be done before planting, or planting may be done first and then the plot cleared. Trees and other vegetation are cut down on top of the newly planted crops. The cut material slowly starts to rot. It provides mulch. The new plantings grow up through the mulch.

The traditional slash-and-mulch system has real benefits in high-rainfall, tropical places. The mulching process helps conserve the soil. You need a lot of mulch, so the system only works where there is still plenty of forest and fallow time. Here is what the mulch does:

- It covers up weeds and makes it very hard for them to grow.
- It protects the soil from erosion by heavy rainfall and keeps the soil cooler in hot sunshine.
- It protects the young crop from very heavy rain and wind.
- It allows water to soak into the soil and then helps to keep the soil moist.
- It slowly adds nutrients or natural fertiliser to the soil. This happens as the mulched plants break down, releasing nutrients more slowly than when they are burnt down.

Cutting down trees and plants on top of newly planted crops looks like a mess (or a disaster!). Government officers thought this system killed nearly half of the planting material. But studies have shown that only about five per cent of the new plantings are damaged. The system works. Like some other traditional practices, it was so different from imported systems that it was hard for outsiders to accept its benefits. But this is a case of traditional people adapting a shifting agriculture system to make their work easier and conserve the environment.

OTHER FORMS OF TRADITIONAL CONSERVATION

Traditional cultures in Papua New Guinea had other elements that conserved or protected part of the environment. For example, there are many stories about places where it is unsafe to go. Some of these stories protect people from natural hazards (see Chapter 1).

Tambu

Sometimes people's stories both protect them from a hazard and protect the environment. People in Manus Province, for example, warned anthropologists not to go into a particular cave. They said it was inhabited by evil spirits and it was *tambu* to go in. The anthropologists thought it was just a story and went into the cave to explore. All got very sick from disease carried by bats in the cave, and at least one died.

A single tree, a place or a much larger area can be tambu. *This provides some traditional protection.*

EXPLORE

- Does making a tree *tambu* help preserve that part of the environment?
- What about places that are *tambu*?
- Is this a type of traditional conservation?
- Is *tambu* part of sorcery or something else?
- What is *tambu* in your area? Does this help conserve, preserve or protect the environment?
- Does *tambu* protect property in your area?
- Is *tambu* a tradition for the future or should it be left in the past?

There are many places in Papua New Guinea that people traditionally considered sacred. Access was limited. This worked to protect the environment. And there are often landforms where people take care not to annoy the spirits that are traditionally said to live there. The tops of mountains and the tops of ridges are two examples. People tend to be quiet and careful in these places. Again, this helps conserve the environment.

This is what local landowners call Mount Gefea in the Highlands. Local people tell stories of it being a place to stay away from. According to this tradition, everyone who goes there gets very confused and lost. This type of traditional belief helps to protect this environment. It makes Mount Gefea a reserve that can help restock plants and animals to nearby locations.

EXPLORE

- What traditional stories come from your area that may keep people away from a place?
- Are the stories possibly warning of a natural hazard?
- Are they acting to conserve, preserve or protect the environment?
- Can you find any ways that traditional stories have protected your environment?

GROUPS RELATED TO DIFFERENT ANIMALS OR BIRDS

A further type of traditional conservation is tied directly to another set of traditional belief systems. People who believed they had a relationship to some animal or bird might protect that creature and say it was *tambu* to kill it. For example, the people of Kumbeme village, near Ialibu in Southern Highlands Province, protect the black long-tailed bird of paradise. The bird is associated with the women of this group and that helps its conservation.

The Korafe people of the Tufi area in Oro Province have the sea turtle as a traditional ancestor. Consequently, they do not eat turtle meat. This has made Tufi a place where divers can see more turtles than in other parts of the country.

EXPLORE

- Are there belief systems that protect or conserve any animals, birds or plants in your area?
- How good are these systems for traditional conservation?

TRADITION, CONSERVATION AND THE FUTURE

You can find national and international non-government organisations trying to work with traditional landowners to improve conservation. You can also find government bodies concerned with this at the local, provincial and national level. Overseas governments have also worked to assist conservation in PNG.

Ultimately, the future of conservation and tradition is up to you. There are people across PNG working on these issues.

George Sari is an example of a Papua New Guinean concerned about tradition and conservation. He worries that birds, plants and animals are being lost in land clearing. He tries to express these concerns in his paintings. He does them in his village near Goroka.

He is also concerned about the way some traditions harm women and benefit men. He sees many instances where women do the traditional work and men take the credit. Like many Papua New Guineans, he is searching for what is good in tradition and what should be changed.

Artist George Sari stands in the doorway of his village home to show a painting about traditional life and the rich traditional environment of the past.

EXPLORE

Make a poster or other artwork to tell a story about a traditional way to use or to conserve the environment.

TRADITIONAL SOLUTIONS FOR CONFLICT

Unit 3 Grade 10 includes an exploration of conflict. You can use this part of the unit to explore the question: 'Can tradition teach practical lessons to assist in conflict resolution?' There are various areas you can investigate:

- traditional knowledge about conflict and fighting
- traditional solutions for conflict inside a family
- traditional solutions for wider conflicts between larger groups or between traditional enemies.

TRADITIONAL KNOWLEDGE ABOUT CONFLICT AND FIGHTING

Fight leaders and fighting have a long history in Papua New Guinea. People fought each other over land and its resources. Some groups sent fighters long distances to raid villages for brides and heads.

Any study of traditional conflict should be done as a comparison between PNG and other places and conflicts. Fighting is a universal problem.

It is easy to see this as something special about Papua New Guinea. But a study of any people around the world will show that there has been violence and conflict everywhere. Study the international section of any newspaper to see how difficult the problems of conflict are.

The lessons you may be able to learn from traditional conflict are the ways to stop it. We will look at some of them here. You can then explore your area for people who help bring peace to conflict.

TRADITIONAL SOLUTIONS FOR CONFLICT INSIDE A FAMILY

The concept of family varies greatly, depending on the tradition. In some places the concept may hardly have applied. Certainly males were counted on to defend their families from attack. That type of inter-group conflict we look at in the final section.

Traditionally people have always tried to keep the peace in family groups. For example, the Tawala people are a cultural group in Milne Bay. This is a matrilineal culture in which land ownership rests with women. Like all peoples, they could have severe family fights. A woman could stop a fight between two male family members (brothers or cousins). But she would only intervene if no other male member of the family could stop the fight. She did this as the last chance for peace. She would take off the inner grass skirt she was wearing and toss it onto the ground. The power of this act and article of clothing stopped the fight. The fighters then had to pay the woman. They would kill a pig for her.

Compensation inside a family is one way to solve a serious family conflict. This may be formal or informal where one family member gives compensation to another.

EXPLORE

- What traditional knowledge can you find for settling or avoiding family conflicts?
- Question the older people in your area. Can they give examples of how family conflict was settled traditionally?

Not shaming a person was an important way to prevent conflict. For example, a number of traditional cases are recorded in which a husband shamed his wife and she committed suicide by jumping from a coconut tree or drinking derris root. (In Kiribati today, shame in families is a trigger for suicide by teenage boys and young men. In all Pacific cultures, shame is a powerful force.)

Domestic violence was common in traditional male–female relations. In some PNG cultures, women could fight back. But this really did not stop conflict. In various places, a woman's male relatives might protect her or take her back from an abusive male partner. The male relatives had to be powerful. Removing a sister from her partner could also involve conflict. In almost all cases of dissolving the partnership, a woman's relatives had to pay back the bride price.

The whole system of bride price has been questioned. It may have caused a man to think of his female partner as a commodity.

Domestic violence was common between males and females.

EXPLORE

- What are the consequences of paying a bride price?
- Does it trap women in relationships with domestic violence?
- Does it make men think they own a woman?
- What is the situation with bride price in your area?

TRADITIONAL SOLUTIONS FOR CONFLICT BETWEEN LARGER GROUPS OR TRADITIONAL ENEMIES

COMPENSATION

Most traditional communities in Papua New Guinea did not have a system of chiefs. Each generation had its own leaders. This made rules very flexible. You saw in Chapter 4 that traditional leadership was based on what people saw as fair and just. Each conflict was judged

Conflict is resolved through discussion and payment of compensation.

separately and had different solutions applied. This made traditional conflict resolution very flexible. There were no fixed rules.

This also made some conflicts very difficult to resolve. One party might say they wanted peace and then immediately kill the other person. Each generation worked to resolve some conflicts, and many leaders kept a long list of past problems for use in negotiating compensation.

Agreeing on compensation has long been the traditional way to stop conflict between two groups. Leaders will spend hours or days going over past history. (And if they are not careful, this can make some people so angry that they start fighting again.) Both sides will present their case. If conflict resolution is successful, compensation will be agreed and paid.

EXPLORE

- How important is compensation in your area?
- Is it helping to resolve conflict?
- Does it provide an incentive for more conflict?
- What different types of compensation ceremonies can you record for your area?

OTHER TRADITIONAL WAYS TO PREVENT OR STOP CONFLICT

SHAME ON A LARGER SCALE

With conflict between larger groups, not shaming people was a good way to prevent conflict. For example, if a host group put on such a big feast that their guests knew they could not pay it back with a similar feast, the shame of this could lead to war. In this case, not shaming another group could mean putting on a feast that the invited group could reciprocate. In other words, after attending the feast the guests knew that next time they would be able to produce a similar feast to pay back their hosts.

FAIRNESS

Within communities, people saw good leaders as those who treated everyone fairly. Allocating land rights and land use in a manner people thought was fair helped keep the peace. Again, in the shifting system of new leaders with every generation, what was considered fair or unfair could change. A wise leader was fair and flexible to avoid conflict.

TREATING PEOPLE GENEROUSLY

Being too generous could shame someone. But treating people generously is a traditional value. It often prevented conflict and continues to be an important value in many places.

AVOIDING CONFRONTATION

Another way of traditionally preventing conflict was to avoid confrontation. People kept away from each other or did not react when someone did something that might make them angry.

MARRIAGE AND CHILD EXCHANGE

Marriages between groups could help to build networks and stop conflict between them. Some men have adapted this traditional strategy to build a political power base through multiple marriages.

Another way to strengthen relations between groups or within communities was child exchanges. This is where one family gave a child or children to newly married couples or to couples who had trouble conceiving. Both marriage and child exchange worked to strengthen relationships and so reduce the potential for conflict.

EXPLORE

Look at the ways conflicts are solved in your area. This means you will have to ask people about the history of conflicts. You may find a number of conflicts that have not been resolved. You should also find some that have been solved. Start with these. Then you can move to unresolved conflict. For conflicts that have been resolved:

- Did any part of traditional knowledge or practice help stop the conflict?
- If so, record how it worked.
- What other types of knowledge or practice helped?
- Again, if so, record how it worked.
- What lessons can you learn from conflicts that have been resolved? Make a list.
- From these lessons, what might help the conflicts that are not resolved?

USING TRADITIONAL KNOWLEDGE TO HELP A COMMUNITY PROJECT

Unit 4, Grade 10 is a five-week unit involving a community project. It gives a five-step process for doing a community project. You can use traditional knowledge as part of the mix when completing the project.

THE FIVE-STEP PROCESS FOR A COMMUNITY PROJECT

You can find details for the five-step process in the Grade 10 Social Science textbook produced by Oxford University Press. Here is a quick review of it. The times spent on each part can vary; they are only suggestions.

Step 1 Identify a community project that will help the community and its resources (week one)
Step 2 Plan for the project (weeks one and two)
Step 3 Test your plan (week two)
Step 4 Do the community project (weeks three and four)
Step 5 Review the results (week five)

QUESTIONS ABOUT TRADITIONAL KNOWLEDGE

You have looked at what has been of value in the past. You have looked at how past tradition might link to the present and the future. This can help you to answer the question, 'Who are you?' and for Papua New Guinea, 'Who are we?' You could use the same approach to a community project.

Let's look at ideas for using traditional knowledge as part of a community project. There are two questions to start with:

1. What type of projects might use traditional knowledge to benefit communities?
2. What are the incentives or reasons for a community to use traditional knowledge today?

OVERVIEW: TRADITIONAL KNOWLEDGE AND CASH

The biggest change to most traditional knowledge in Papua New Guinea comes from mixing in cash. Everyone now needs some money. Traditional knowledge, skills and resources may contribute in different ways to community well-being as people adapt to a cash society. Below are three possible areas where traditional knowledge can contribute.

1 IMPROVING OPPORTUNITIES TO EARN CASH

One possible theme for a community project would be to help improve ways people can earn cash for traditional knowledge, skills and resources. There are at least two major areas for this type of project:

- improving existing activities
- reviving traditions for cash.

Improving existing activities

Everywhere in PNG, you can find existing activities using traditional knowledge, skills and resources. Here are some ideas about projects that might assist people in a community.

1. **Marketing.** Most traditional items for sale receive very little or no marketing. Simple marketing involves letting people know about a product. (For example: what it costs, how it is made, what it represents.) Look at the pictures on the next page.

   Consider these questions about places like the ones in the photos:

   - Is there any simple way to improve their marketing? How can more people come to know about their products? Or better: how can more people who are likely to buy this type of traditional craft be made aware of where they are sold in the community?
   - Is there any way places like these can advertise without large cost?
   - Would advertising work?
   - Is there any way to tell more possible buyers about this place?

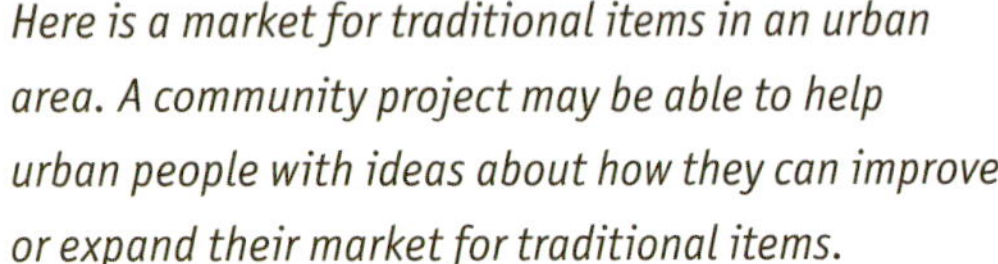

Here is a market for traditional items in an urban area. A community project may be able to help urban people with ideas about how they can improve or expand their market for traditional items.

Here is an example of a village selling items based on traditional knowledge, skills and resources. Could a community project help this type of activity too? You would have to explore and discuss to find out.

EXPLORE

Look at your own community:

- Are people around you trying to sell some traditional craft or artefact?
- How do they market their product?
- Is there any way for more people to learn about the product?
- Is there any way to attract more people to see the product?

QUESTIONS TO HELP WITH MARKETING TRADITIONAL KNOWLEDGE, SKILLS AND RESOURCES

For any community marketing project, you will need to interview both sellers and buyers (or people who might become buyers).

You will need to interview *sellers*. Find out what they think would help them sell more. You will need to question them about their supplies, their products, the skills they are using and the problems they are having.

You will also need to find out what appeals to *buyers*:

- What are they looking for?
- What types of traditional artefacts appeal to them?
- What about quality?
- What about size and weight?
- What about safety in the marketplace (or safety getting to the marketplace)?
- What about cleanliness?
- In general, is the marketplace an environment the buyer wants to be in?

2 **Conditions at the market.** Another community project could be to look at conditions in marketplaces run by local or provincial authorities. The simplest community project would be to organise a clean-up day. You would need teacher supervision and coordination with authorities.

A community project with a local market could be as simple as a clean-up day or could involve making longer-term changes.

You could expand this to organise a community project to make longer-term improvements. Many markets selling traditional foods and other items suffer neglect. A community project could look at reasons for this. You could explore ways to improve the market environment.

Many people sell traditional products to the community. They take pride and present their goods as best they can. Each person is doing a good job, but the larger market may need help. This is another possible area for a community project.

Surveying market users. Again, you would need to talk to buyers, sellers and authorities. First you would need to survey the problems with people using the market. Is the market:

- dirty?
- dusty?
- muddy?
- often flooded?
- poorly maintained?
- safe for buyers?
- accessible?
- a place with conflict problems?
- other?

You would need to determine what the buyers, sellers and authorities believe are the major problems. Then you can work on one or two of the top problems.

Possible solutions. You can then explore different solutions. These might include answering questions such as these:

- Are there ways to change official attitudes about traditional markets?
- Are there ways to have communities take pride in improving their markets?
- Are there ways to have authorities provide funding for market improvements?

Sometimes you might find officials have a bias or prejudice against traditional markets and sellers. You will need to work carefully to understand why this is so. You will need to find ways to change these biases or prejudices.

Reviving traditions for cash

Another possible community project to use traditional knowledge, skills and resources in a cash society could involve reviving knowledge that is not being used. This type of project would explore opportunities from the past.

Here are some types of questions that could be used to see if this kind of community project is possible:

- Are there artefacts that are disappearing from common use that might be of interest to buyers?
- With the mineral and gas boom, are there possible buyers for artefacts that have stopped being made?
- Do the knowledge, skills and resources still exist to be revived?
- Can these items be revived for a cash value?

2 SAVINGS: USING TRADITION TO MAKE SAVINGS

Using traditional knowledge, skills and resources may save people money. Growing your own food, constructing your own bed or collecting your own fuel are all ways people can save money.

This can happen at a social level. Working together, helping each other to build a house or provide security, is another way people save on cash. Tradition can help save or conserve cash. You will see examples of this all around you.

One possible community project would be to audit or investigate possible ways people could use traditional knowledge, skills and resources to save money. In some communities there may be opportunities for this. In other communities, people may already be fully using their traditional resources.

For a savings community project, you would explore and act on questions like these:

- Are there food trees or other traditional resources that can be planted?
- Are there any ways to help people further use traditional knowledge, skills and resources to help them save cash?
- What could a class community project do to help the community save through using traditional resources?

Another approach would be to look at *diet*. For example, leafy greens are important for good health. They provide minerals and vitamins. People on high-carbohydrate and high-fat diets may be missing out on good health. A project that looked at growing and using traditional greens would be a way to assist healthy living. Good health is important and saves on health costs.

3 CONSERVATION AND CASH

In this textbook you have found references to mountains as special forest reserves. In some places now, mountains are the last reserves of forest. There are other areas of forest too, but Papua New Guinea has lost much of its easily accessible forest. Deforestation is a major problem. People want cash, so they are willing to sell their forests. At the same time, many traditional beliefs have helped conserve forests, especially forests on mountains.

One promise that floats over the forests of Papua New Guinea is the *carbon storage value* of forests (see box on the next page). Global warming is continuing. More nations now worry about having too much carbon dioxide in the world's atmosphere. This problem will only grow in the future.

Carbon credits may be one way to help conserve forests and bring cash into the community.

Ideas and schemes are being proposed to use the selling of carbon credits to save forests. This is like being paid compensation to keep the forest. The situation is constantly changing. It is an area to research for possible community benefits.

WHAT IS CARBON STORAGE VALUE?

A major reason for global warming is humans adding carbon dioxide to the atmosphere. Burning coal and other fossil fuels is one way to do this. Land clearing is another way. Nations that do these things on a large scale are contributing to global warming.

These nations can slow or stop some of these activities. Or they may pay another country to store carbon dioxide. They would buy carbon credits from that country to 'offset' (balance) the carbon dioxide they put in the atmosphere.

This is where forests come in. Forests are important for storing carbon dioxide. Trees and plants store it as they grow. Their value for storing carbon is high.

This leads to the idea of countries buying carbon credits from people who keep their forests and do not cut them down. This type of carbon storage could make forests more valuable by not cutting them. PNG landowners could keep their forests and earn cash. It is almost certain to happen in the future. You will need to follow current events and talk to NGOs to see what the latest information is.

The five weeks available for your community project limits you. If you wanted to explore carbon credits, you would need to discuss the situation with both non-government organisations (NGOs) and government officials. In the time you have, probably the best you could do would be to educate landowners.

This type of project might include the following:

- You could search out information from different sources.
- You could evaluate that information.
- You could provide landowners and others in the community with the latest information about carbon credits for forest conservation.
- You could help landowners understand what carbon credits may mean to them.
- You could help improve landowners' knowledge about different NGOs and government officials.
- You could educate people on where they could continue to get reliable information.
- You might suggest ways landowners could work as a group to continue to get information and to act on carbon credits and the distribution of the benefits. (But remember, project time is limited.)

Eventually some form of global carbon market will function. This will make conserving forests easier. It will give the landowners cash to protect the forests. Alerting the community to what is happening can help them with decisions about what they will do with forest resources. Collecting traditional knowledge and beliefs may help them to conserve this resource. Combining these two activities could be a community project.

TRADITIONAL KNOWLEDGE, SKILLS AND RESOURCES HISTORY

A COMMUNITY PROJECT THAT DOES NOT INVOLVE CASH

Many Papua New Guineans worry about traditions that are being lost. Stories, skills, knowledge and some resources are vanishing. You may find people in the community who want to make a record of this knowledge so it is not completely lost.

A possible community project would be to record traditional knowledge by writing down what people knew and did in the past. Drawings or photos could be used to explain what was done or how objects and resources worked. They could also explain traditional social relationships and activities.

Collecting a history of community knowledge like this could include any area. For example:

- what people thought, their beliefs and values
- what stories they had
- how they used different parts of the environment
- how they interacted.

Specialist carving is vanishing in some places.

Traditional scar practices and tattoos have disappeared or are starting to disappear in some parts of Papua New Guinea.

You could look around your community:

- What skills and knowledge are disappearing?
- Can you make a record of how they were done in the past?
- What was their importance?
- How were they used?
- What meanings did they have or do they still have?

You would need to choose just one subject. Then you would carefully record all the information you could find about it. To keep this information for future generations, you could make copies for:

1. your school library
2. the National Library of PNG in Port Moresby
3. some other PNG university library.

It is good to have copies in different places. This increases the chances of your information being preserved and used in the future. Check with your teachers. Make a plan to deliver a copy with a cover that clearly states what it is and provides collection information (see next page).

TRADITIONAL PAPUA NEW GUINEA INFORMATION ABOUT

____

Collected at:

a. Place: ____________________

b. District: ____________________

c. Province: ____________________

Collection dates: ______________________________________

[give the time period and dates the material was collected]

Collected by: ______________________________________

[include the names of everyone who collected and wrote up the project]

Collected from the following people: ______________________________________

[include the names of everyone who provided information unless they specifically ask not to have their name used]

[You will need to explore methods to get a copy of your information to a library. Maybe you can find a trusted person to hand-deliver your material.]

ACKNOWLEDGMENTS

The author and the publisher wish to thank the following copyright holders for reproduction of their material.

Alamy/imagebroker, p.19 (bottom) /jeremy sutton-hibbert, p.20 /Michael Patrick O'Neill, p.99; **Bradshaw Foundation, Geneva**, p.41 (top); © **The Trustees of the British Museum**, p.58 (bottom); **Daniel Evans**/The World Bank, p.27 (top); **Dreamstime.com**/Smithore, p.17; **Getty Images**/AFP, p.101 /Gerry Ellis, pp.96, 112 /Jill Ferry, Cover /Tim Laman, p.18; **Integrity of Political Parties & Candidates Commission**, p.51; **Jon Irvine via Flickr**, p.44; **Michael Johnson via Flickr**, p.35; **NASA**, p.22; **Photoshot**/NHPA, p.65; **shutterstock**, pp.15, 46, 57, 58 (top), 67 (top), 73, 88; **Simeon Telfer via Flickr**, p.10 (bottom); **Visuals Unlimited**/James Beveridge, p.68; **Stephen Ranck**, all other editorial images.

Every effort has been made to trace the original source of copyright material contained in this book. The publisher will be pleased to hear from copyright holders to rectify any errors or omissions.